MARITAL

COUNSELING

SUCCESSFUL PASTORAL COUNSELING SERIES

MARITAL
COUNSELING

R. LOFTON HUDSON

Prentice-Hall, Inc., Englewood Cliffs, N.J.

HQ10
H8

Marital Counseling
by R. Lofton Hudson

55706–T

Prentice-Hall International, Inc.
(*London, Tokyo, Sydney, Paris*)
Prentice-Hall of Canada, Ltd.

Printed in the United States of America

Third printing. . . . . . . April, 1966

DEDICATION

To my wife, who for thirty years has generously shared the time she deserved with those who needed help in marital problems.

INTRODUCTION

This series of books represents the most comprehensive publishing effort ever made in the field of pastoral care. These books could not have been published twenty-five years ago, or probably even ten, for the material was not then available. In the past, single books have been available covering different phases of the task. Now we are bringing the subjects together in a single series. Here we present a library of pastoral care covering the major topics and problems that most pastors will encounter in their ministry. Fortunately, not all of these problems need be faced every week or even every month. But, when they are, the minister wants help and he wants it immediately.

These books are prepared for the non-specialized minister serving the local church, where he is the most accessible professional person in the community. It is a well accepted fact that more people turn to clergy when in trouble than to all other professional people. Therefore, the pastor must not fail them.

Russell L. Dicks
General Editor

PREFACE

My aim has been to keep an eye on the two people who come to the counselor rather than merely look into the books for analyses of what is wrong in modern marriages. This is not to disparage what has been written. Much of it has been of great value, but the best way to learn about people is from people.

For 25 years I have wrestled with the interpersonal relations of marital problems. One criterion of therapy has been kept in mind: what works and what does not. "Works" refers to the decisions which result from marriage counseling so two people can look back upon them with satisfaction five or ten years afterwards. This seems to be a reasonable criterion. Success can never be predicated on what the marriage counselor thinks is the correct decision, on the number of people who decide not to divorce, or upon what the church or community thinks.

The goal of marriage counseling is that two people will come to know themselves better, to understand how their marriage ran into a roadblock and to find a way around or decide to go back to the place where they were enjoying each other. Sometimes there is no road back. Too many chuck holes have been developed. In such cases, especially if there are children involved, these situations leave us sad. We still must stand by the proposition that two people must find their own best alternatives with whatever insights the counselor and the counselees, working together, may achieve.

It is hoped that this volume may be of help to all who attempt to guide those who have marriage problems. Clergymen, physicians and social workers will doubtless be the primary users of this material. In our culture, however, many people counsel in marriage difficulties. All of these, I trust, will be aided by what they find herein.

9

CONTENTS

MARITAL

COUNSELING

ONE

The PASTOR As

MARRIAGE COUNSELOR

"Today the nation's 350,000 clergymen are undoubtedly seeing more people 'clinically' than all the psychiatrists, psychologists and psychoanalysts combined." These are the words of Dr. O. Hobart Mowrer, research professor in the Department of Psychology of the University of Illinois.[1]

We may well consider why people now turn to their pastors for help with family problems. Formerly, people turned to their parents for help when the going got rough. With the changing concepts of family life, the trend is for a couple to feel proud of standing on their own without having to seek help—or even advice—from their parents.

Also, professional counselors advise against turning to in-laws and other relatives. And, in our mobile and highly industrialized society a large percentage of Americans move away from their parents and rarely see them except for occasional, perhaps annual, visits.

Where, then, do people under stress find a parent-figure? The physician is usually too busy, but the pastor is in an ideal position. I use the term *parent-figure*, but it should be kept in mind that this is an all-embracing image. Which aspect of parental function does an adult look for in the pastor? Certainly not provider, or chauffeur or authoritarian controller. Here the concept of role almost ceases to be of value, because of its ambiguity and complexity.

Concept of role means that in our lives, particularly in our early lives, we see people perform certain duties and act toward us in a certain way. We come to expect this behavior from them. Roles are what people are in their relation to us. Roles always involve the fulfilling of some need or wish. They are patterns of behavior that are somewhat predictable and are seen by us, in the case of favorable roles, as desirable or necessary.

There are many roles in which people may cast the minister.

[1] Editorial in *Academy Reporter*, Vol. 3, No. 8 (November 1958).

These parts may be desirable neither from his standpoint nor from theirs—if we hold that autonomous, self-directing individuals are one of our goals in religion. Some people see their pastor as the parent who gives final answers on all matters of action; the policeman who watches to see if people are doing anything wrong; the friend upon whom they may impose anytime they wish; the superman who never makes a mistake (a little child's conception of his father); a kind of saint who will sacrifice all for anyone; a genius who has all the answers, and a religious giant who can, with God's help, perform miracles. All of these conceptions are naive and grow out of immature thinking and feeling about religion and its place in life.

Without attempting to define how the minister sees his role or how this role is changing in our culture, let us look at the specific aspects that apply to marriage problems. Here again, the self-concept of the minister and that of the layman may be somewhat at variance. We shall try, however, to describe the role-images that would be largely agreed upon in our culture.

The minister is a friend-at-large for the church and God. He goes to see people when they need him—in hospitals, in their homes and even in jails. Most ministers are "on call" day or night seven days a week. It is assumed that he has genuine concern for all people and especially for those who are in trouble. While he cannot be expected to be able to meet every need—physical, financial or even emotional—he will probably know who in the community can furnish a working approach to these special needs.

No one else in our culture has precisely this role. Probably the nearest to it is that of the policeman or the physician.

The minister is sincerely interested in marriage and the home. In many communions, he baptizes the babies when they are born and pledges the parents or godparents to bring them up in "the nurture and admonition of the Lord." He performs the marriage ceremonies. Often he gives premarital guidance. The ceremony itself includes words of direction about how the partners should relate to each other and what a home should be like. When the child is old enough to be taught the meaning of personal faith, the minister is the one who leads in this instruction. Not infrequently these duties take him into the homes of his parishioners.

In sermons and lectures, the minister, whether or not he ever preaches a "series" on the home, cannot help but apply the Christian teachings to family life. He sets forth ideals about right and wrong as they relate to Sabbath observance, social customs, personal habits and family worship.

Here is a man who has some ideas, at least, about how things ought to be in a marriage. It is natural for people to turn to him with a marraige problem.

The minister is in a trusted role as far as divorce issues are concerned. Trusted by whom? By those who believe that divorce should not occur in this given case and perhaps even by the general public who knows that, by-and-large, ministers will try to save a marriage, if possible. The views of ministers will range from the firm stand that "there is no such thing as divorce in God's sight" to the more flexible viewpoint that two people ought to live together only if they are each fulfilling themselves reasonably well in this relationship—and the interpretation of "reasonably well" will be left up to the individuals involved.

The Christian ideal that one woman should be married to one man for life would, in itself, tend to put the minister in a trusted role on the divorce issue—at least by people who do not wish marriages to end in divorce. Usually people who turn for marriage counseling to any professional person have some hope that the marriage can be helped. Sometimes, only one of the spouses wishes to save the marriage. Even here, the minister may be able to console the one who is deserted with the idea that there is a way of life ahead and help him or her to find it. He may even—if his skills and insights are sufficient—help the abandoned one to understand why it happened.

The minister is considered an authority on right and wrong. Again a question: Considered by whom? Usually by those who turn to him. He is thought by most people to be a conservative on morals.

If a wife reports that her husband insists on mouth-genital sexual play, she will probably expect the minister to see this as some kind of perversion. If a man says, "My wife is having an affair with her boss," he can be very sure that the minister will not say, "So what? It happens all the time."

The role-expectation presupposes that the minister is the defender of such values as: chastity; self-giving within the marriage; justice and fairness in such matters as money; self-control in handling anger; unselfishness in relation to children and in-laws, etc. He can usually be expected to have opinions on what makes a good marriage and a good home atmosphere.

The minister offers some kind of salvation. I refer here to the fact that religion proposes to bring into our lives a power and help that is beyond ourselves.

When marriages are failing, individuals often are faced with their own inadequacies. They may begin to ask themselves, "What is wrong with me?" Everyone knows that religion attempts to tell us what is wrong with us and how we can right that which is wrong— how we can be "saved."

Sometimes an individual may feel that the trouble is solely with the mate. What is wrong with her? Maybe religion can help. They know that religion proposes to change people. "If I can get her to talk to her minister, maybe he can straighten her out," the husband may say to himself.

The role is not a bad one, from the minister's standpoint. He does offer faith, hope and love as the way out of our immaturities. Confession, prayer, Bible reading, worship and many other means are used to the ends of finding God and finding ourselves. Increasingly, counseling is added to these means of finding both ourselves and our deepest relationships with both God and man.

A young dental student had been married three years to a girl one year younger than himself. Their only child was one year old. In anger and resentment, she left him one night and returned to her home. When she learned that he was concerned enough to turn to a marriage counselor, she returned to her spouse and came in for an interview.

At a particular point in the interviews he told me that on their wedding night his wife got on her knees beside her bed to pray as she had been accustomed to. To him, this was hilarious. He laughed and told her how ridiculous it was. Having been reared in a non-religious home, he did not know that this sort of thing happened.

Later he asked me, "What in the world does a person do about his anger?"

"I pray about mine," I said simply.

"You may be surprised to know that I have been trying to pray, but I feel like I am talking to myself. Is that normal? Do other people feel that way about prayer?"

I explained that often we who have been Christians for years feel a long way from God. I encouraged him to be specific in what he asked of God and not to be surprised if God answered his prayer. I loaned him a copy of the J. B. Phillips' translation of the Gospels, which had just been published.

A few weeks later he filled out a membership application card in a church. In a follow-up two years later, he reported that they were happy together—and now attended church every Sunday.

Looking back, I believe that he turned to me because of my role as a minister-counselor. However, I do not believe he would have made the progress he has made without religious faith, as expressed first in personal prayer.

One of the distinctive assets that the pastor has is his access to the home. If he knows there is a marriage problem he may find it difficult to go directly to the couple and confront them with the fact. It may be wholly inadvisable for him to do so, even if well-meaning friends request it. But he can make himself available. He can build a relationship with the family in order to make it easy for them to turn to him in times of trouble.

Sometimes he can say to a wife, "John seems to be losing interest in the church; I wonder if he would have lunch with me some day so we can get a little better acquainted." Or, "I wonder if he will come by my study sometime and see if we can talk about the problem." Any pastor with tact and good common sense can figure out a way to get to know a parishioner better so the parishioner will feel secure enough to reveal his real spiritual and personal problems.

THE MINISTER EVALUATES HIS LIABILITIES

But the pastor has liabilities in counseling also, particularly in marriage counseling. These should be faced frankly by both the pastor and by those who may refer people to him.

A primary problem in the pastor's marriage counseling is his own training. Most clergymen have read widely in the field of pastoral counseling. But counseling techniques cannot be learned out of a book.

Counseling can be learned best under supervision by those experienced in the field and by direct experience in counseling.

Most pastors can find a college or university near their parish where they can take psychology courses in child or adolescent psychology, personality development, abnormal psychology or social psychology; or sociology courses in family life, anthropology and interpersonal relations. Courses in guidance and counseling may be available at a university or modern seminary. Many mental and general hospitals offer training in counseling in various types of problems under chaplaincy supervision. The carry-over into marriage counseling is of real significance.

If approached properly, most clinical psychologists, psychiatrists and professional marriage counselors are willing to "sell" one hour a week to the pastor to go over his counseling cases with him. This enables the pastor to increase his knowledge of personality problems within the particular contexts that come up in interviews. This, in addition to a period of personal psychotherapy, is the most valuable type of preparation for more effective marriage counseling.

A second problem that the pastor faces is that of his own moral reputation.   If he is called by a wife who is upset over her marriage, and if he visits her home frequently, there is the risk of gossip. Neighbors may suspect that he is "carrying on" with the wife. To avoid such a risk, subsequent interviews, after the first or second, might wisely be held at his home or at his study where someone else may be present in the adjoining office.

Even with such precautions, the pastor may face an irate husband who resents the pastor's discussing intimate personal problems with his wife. Or, if he talks to a husband, the wife may spread the report that he is giving approval to her husband's misbehavior, or is encouraging him in his effort to get a divorce or is meddling in their personal lives. If he encourages a couple to spend less time with their in-laws, he may be accused of breaking the family ties.

In cases of divorce the pastor is in a particularly difficult spot. If the counseling period ends in divorce for the couple, there are always those who are looking for someone to blame, and the counselor is an excellent target. If he sympathizes with one of the troubled marital partners, he may be accused of taking sides.

A third major problem involves that of ethics or values. The pastor cannot avoid facing ethical dilemmas in marriage problems which would stagger the most astute philosophers. An attempt on his part to be non-directive and permissive is not the answer. He has positive ethical values or he would not be in the ministry. He has been trained to evaluate human living by norms which he believes are based on the divine-human encounter and on the revelation of God in Jesus Christ.

It should be pointed out that pastors tend to lean in one of three directions in their concepts of right and wrong concerning marriage problems: (1) they may stand on the pronouncements of their denominations on such questions as divorce and remarriage; (2) they may adopt a legalistic view, cite Scripture passages to prove their points, and insist that those who do not accept their interpretations are living in sin before God, or (3) they may try to get behind the literal interpretations of specific texts and see the great ethical principles that throw light on the particular human situation.

The first two positions seem to me to be very inadequate. The reason is evident to those who have dealt with a great many complex marriage problems. Neither denominational creeds and pronouncements nor literalistic interpretations of the Bible cover adequately the varied complex situations that confront the pastor in marriage counseling. For example, if one says that divorce is justified only in case of adultery, what is the pastor, within that theological framework, to say to the woman who is married to the confirmed homosexual who loathes the female body and refuses to touch her? Should one insist that a woman stay married to a man who carries on sexual play with their nine-year-old daughter and refuses psychiatric treatment? Would one forbid remarriage to a man who was formerly married to a woman who persistently wrote bad checks, indulged in excessive drinking or took dope? To take such a position places the pastor in very much the same position as the Pharisees of the New Testament when they did not see that the Sabbath was made for man and not man for the Sabbath.

If the pastor should take the position that he will merely read the word of God and let them decide for themselves, he is hardly being helpful. The very reason many of these people turn to the pastor is that they are trying to think through the very puzzling discrepancy between what they know as the ideal, as presented in the Bible, and the actual, as presented by their human situation. If they are sincere, they will have asked themselves many times what God would have them do. To send them away without having looked at all facets of their complex situation in the light of what kind of a Father our God is; what the total revelation of His will seems to be concerning how to face such a human problem, and what the future of our relationship with Him may be, is hardly Christian counseling.

The ethical frame of reference that seems to me to be more applicable to marriage counseling would be that of looking behind the specific Scriptures for the principles involved. Marriage is the ideal way of self-fulfillment for most humans—"It is not good for man to be alone" (Gen. 2:18). One woman should be married to one man for life. Their union should be founded upon a considered choice by the two individuals involved, and developed in the spirit of interdependence, self-giving and all the other phases of love. The persons involved and any children of their union are to be valued above tradition, public opinion, family pride or any other external factors. Whatever destroys the individuals or their children is unholy.

However, the application of these principles is not simple. Suppose the marriage seems to be destroying one mate, but not the other? What becomes of human freedom if a man is determined to hold on to his wife, although she has no wish to see him or have him touch her? What is to be said for the rights and the welfare of children when both parents are bickering and destroying each other emotionally?

It is evident to even a casual reader of the Bible that such cases are not dealt with within the Scriptures. There cannot be enough written laws to cover all specific cases, as any attorney knows quite well. Each case must be viewed within the broader framework of great ethical principles.

To carry this a step further, the minister cannot help but get involved in the question of *ought*. People expect him, on some basis, to help them find what they ought to do. Yet, all counseling—however we may define it—aims at aiding the counselee to a self-determined resolution of his problem: he must make the decision. What this amounts to, worded a little differently, is that he ought to make his decision. Even this premise involves other *ought*'s. He ought not allow his attorney or his parents or anyone else to make his decisions for him.

It is often overlooked, however, that we cannot say "You ought" unless we can say "You can," and prior to either of these statements there must be some appraisal of "What do you wish to do?" The correlation of *wish* (or *want*) and *can* and *ought* is the real problem of any kind of action. It does not make sense to say that a person ought to do something, if he cannot do it. Nor does it make sense to talk to people about what they ought to do if they have no desire to do it, or cannot find it within themselves to wish to do it. Here the pastor emerges from his traditional position to the modern role of pastoral counselor. The one is based on moralistic or ethical commands; the other, fully aware of reality factors—including the will of God, tries to bring to bear on the situation whatever sociological, psychological and spiritual factors may influence decisions.

This does not mean that counseling consists of analyzing dynamics, intellectualizing about motivation or explaining why people behave as they do. Here, T. S. Eliot's words are particularly applicable:

I don't want you to make yourself responsible for me;
It's only another kind of contempt.
And I do not want you to explain me to myself.
You're still trying to invent a personality for me.
Which will only keep me away from myself.[2]

In marriage counseling the minister hears the story of the predicament that two people face. He gets something of the background of their present problems. He explores what each wishes, or thinks he wishes, to do about the immediate situation. Interwoven with the dialogue will be the three factors: *wish, can* and *ought*. The *ought* must be what the counselee comes to feel is his, not what the minister thinks or feels. The minister has his *ought*; the counselee must find his own.

A final problem—there are many others, but these seem predominant—*that the minister faces in marriage counseling is that people tend to turn to him and dump their problems in his lap, with a kind of here-it-is-do-something-about-it attitude.* Many people expect magic or miracle, especially from a minister, since the founder of our religion stated that "with God all things are possible" (Matt. 19:26).

It is true that by faith human beings can accomplish more than they can by their own strength alone. Mountains of irresponsibility, doubt, fear and hate are often removed. But, God's power is limited

[2] T. S. Eliot, *The Cocktail Party* (New York: Harcourt, Brace and World, Inc., 1950), p. 98.

by man's disbelief and man's stubbornness. There is God's will and power to be taken into consideration. But there is also, sometimes opposed to God's will, man's free choice—his decisions—to be reckoned with.

Often someone says to the minister, "Do you think there is hope for us to work out our problem if we will both come to see you?" The best answer is: "I do not know. It will depend on how much both of you wish to save the marriage; how patient you both are in gaining insights into the complexity of the problem, and how capable each of you is in making the necessary changes."

Just as the minister takes responsibility not for saving people but only of giving witness to the saving grace of God, so in counseling he takes the responsibility not for saving a marriage but only for providing a relationship where two people can understand themselves better and learn better ways of relating to each other.

TWO

INTERPERSONAL COMPETENCE
In The FAMILY

Any counselor operates within one or more theoretical frameworks of psychotherapy. The minister may choose his own from his training or reading or his own background or experience. The wider his reading the better. He may vary in his handling of different types of people. He should, in fact. But almost inevitably his approach to most problems will be within some system of thought that may be classified as psychology and sociology.

What, then, is the purpose of a "theoretical framework"? In rearing a child, in managing a business, in leading a church or in counseling with a married couple who are thinking of divorce, a human being must operate on theories or viewpoints. He must, consciously or unconsciously, relate to people in terms of what he thinks makes them tick.

What do people need most? What determines their personality? What types of experiences cause them to progress or regress? How does a boy become the kind of man who can be a good husband and a good father? How does a girl become the kind of woman who can be a good wife and mother? How does a human being who is confused and faced with difficult dilemmas resolve them with decisions that will be satisfactory for the remainder of his life?

In marriage counseling we cannot help but have some kind of "theoretical framework." The belief that problems of husband-wife relationships can be solved by the husband's being head of the house and the wife's obeying of his orders is one theory or viewpoint. The belief that when the sexual relationship between the two is successful all else falls into place is another theory. The belief that if a man is "right with God" he will be able to solve his marriage problems is another theory. Such theories will be the basis of the marriage counselor's considerations in discussing problems with a couple.

The counseling process, the goals of counseling, the counselor's response to the immediate problem—all must be seen according to the counselor's view of what it takes to help two people who are involved in a difficult situation.

What is the aim of the minister in his counseling? What are his goals? He may be trained in client-centered therapy, in psychoanalytic theory, in interpersonal relations (the Harry Stack Sullivan school), in dynamic relationship psychology or phenomenological theory.[1]

He may even create his own theory of human progress. In any case, the minister must decide to adopt some kind of viewpoint that will work. He will, no doubt, adopt a viewpoint that embodies his Christian concepts and is sound, as he sees it, from a psychological or psychiatric viewpoint.

The following proposal for viewing family problems leans strongly toward the interpersonal competence field. The school of psychiatry that was originated by Harry Stack Sullivan and adapted by Nelson N. Foote and Leonard S. Cottrell, Jr., seems to be the most useful to the minister. Its emphasis is on the ability of the individual to cope with the kinds of problems that individuals face in a family situation.*

The interpersonal competence approach attempts to discard such terms as *adjustment*, as implying a settled or static state; *happiness*, as based upon a too nebulous concurrence of compatible traits; *emotional maturity*, as too judgmental and lacking in power to motivate the individuals involved. Rather, competence is the understanding of the components of any interpersonal situation or episode and the attempt to find better ways of reacting to the other person or persons involved.

In other words, in any situation that is unsatisfactory to two people, each must view the situation from the other's perspective; weigh the alternatives; define new goals and invent ways of achieving them, and learn techniques for living together in a more satisfactory manner. This process is never static. What worked yesterday may not work today. Therefore, each episode must be played by ear. Living together is a dynamic process which acknowledges changing people in a changing world.

[1] These are all described in Donald D. Glad's *Operational Values in Psychotherapy* (New York: Oxford University Press, 1959), an excellent summary of theories of personality development.

* See Nelson N. Foote and Leonard S. Cottrell, Jr., *Identity and Interpersonal Competence* (Chicago: The University of Chicago Press, 1955).

Foote and Cottrell's formulation of the components or factors that are inherent in the interpersonal experiences in the family are six: *health, intelligence, empathy, autonomy, judgment* and *creativity*. Without attempting to refute or disparage any of these, I should like to analyze the interaction within the family as consisting of the following six factors: *freedom, autonomy, empathy, flexibility, creativity* and *trust*.

Autonomy and *flexibility* are primarily traits or characteristics of the individual. Others, such as *empathy* and *trust*, are primarily focused on what happens between two people in a face-to-face relationship. The distinction, however, is not clear-cut. "Being" is always "being-with-others." There are no Robinson Crusoes, except in fiction. Fenichel states: "The human being becomes a human being (an ego) by entering into interrelations with other human beings."[2]

In the context of this book, the interpersonal competence approach means that people who have these six qualities will be successful in a close, permanent relationship. Those who lack one or more will fail. In a sense, this means that when we look at a marriage problem we look for the degree of freedom, autonomy, empathy, flexibility, creativity and trust that each has, or doesn't have, and how these affect the relationship.

These components are goals. They are all necessary—in one degree or another—in every good marriage. If someone questions whether they were arrived at empirically or whether they were superimposed on the situation, my only answer would be: "As I have looked at marriage problems and have seen failing marriages become successful ones, these factors seem to be the ones that prominently figure in the change that takes place. There will doubtless be other analyses of interaction that will replace these, but I find no better way of defining success or failure at present. Their usefulness will be proved or disproved by seeing whether or not they fit the cases in hand. This, it would seem, is scientific and good common sense."[3]

The first component of good interpersonal relations in the home is *freedom*.

[2] Otto Fenichel, "Psychoanalytic Remarks on Fromm's Book, *Escape from Freedom*," *The Psychoanalytic Review*, Vol. 31 (1944), p. 139.

[3] See Fritz Heider's *The Psychology of Interpersonal Relations* (New York: John Wiley & Sons, Inc., 1958) for a good defense of "common sense" psychology.

Without freedom, human beings are mere puppets operated by someone else or by some power. The opposite of freedom is compulsion. Nietzsche called freedom the capacity "to become what we truly are." Freedom, then, is the possibility angle of human living. If every individual is to be valuable and respected, he must have a degree of freedom to fulfill himself, even in marriage.

A bound or enslaved person cannot make a good marriage mate. He may be enslaved by prejudices, by custom and convention, by fear, by drink, by subconscious factors or even by religion. He may be said to be bound if the decisions he makes are not largely his own in the light of the best insights he has. In a sense, all of us are somewhat restricted, in that ignorance and false values color our thinking and actions to some extent.

Freedom means the ability to respond to others, to be open to others. In sermons and teaching, the churches rightly couple freedom with responsibility—and "Man is responsible for his own irresponsibility."[4] But how can man be free to respond unless he is in a situation that recognizes freedom and unless he has matured to the point that he will be responsible for himself?

Freedom in a marriage is never absolute. We speak, for instance, of the "marriage bond." Marriage is a state in which two people have accepted certain limitations to their freedom. Being voluntary and somewhat defined, marriage need not leave individuals feeling trapped or enslaved. If two people have committed themselves to a relationship of love and devotedness, they still may have freedom-within-limits and may thereby fulfill themselves.

Any marriage counselor of experience could give a hundred examples of the distortions and perversions of freedom in sick marriages. Here are examples, in the form of direct quotations:

"Don't you think a man has a right to demand that his wife meet his sexual needs, as long as he is not unreasonable?"

"No wife of mine is going to work; the minute she gets a job I quit mine."

"He forces me to ask him for money, even to buy a pair of stockings."

"Every time I play golf or go out with the boys she pitches a fit, so I either get mad or feel guilty."

[4] John Macquarrie, *An Existentialist Theology* (New York: The Macmillan Company, 1955), p. 205.

"I have told her and told her that if she doesn't keep things picked up around the house, I will not come home."

"I can't see what all the fuss is about; I provide for her and the kids and treat them right. Why is she always nagging me to take her out somewhere?"

"We would not have any trouble if he would keep his folks out of it; he never makes a decision without asking his mother."

More could be written about each of these statements and the overtones one hears in them. They have this in common: one mate is trying to compel the other to react according to his or her own wishes.

The marriage counselor must remain alert to methods people use to "get their way." Among them he will find threats, appeals to sympathy, attempts to make the other feel guilty ("Look how much I have done for you"), ridicule, out-talking of the other person and even prayer.

In contrast with these threats to freedom, good marriages are made by two people who recognize that each has his own rights and will, and that one need not dominate the other. There must be response—verbal, affectional and sexual. But even in these areas two people differ a great deal and this difference must be accepted. Some people have a very small core of affectional response; others find their greatest joy in spontaneous self-giving.

For the marriage counselor the important thing is to see how each views the element of freedom; what needs to control or compel each other are present, and how the marriage relation can be reconstructed so that the degree of freedom and response needed can be found. The marriage bed need not be a prison. And relationship is not the same as enslavement.

The second, and probably the most important, component of marriage is *autonomy*. How can there be a relationship unless the individuals are self-directing?

Erich Fromm has thus stated the importance of autonomy:

> It is part of the tragedy of the human situation that the development of the self is never completed; even under the best conditions only part of man's potentialities is realized. Man always dies before he is fully born.[5]

[5] *Man for Himself* (New York: Holt, Rinehart and Winston, Inc., 1947), p. 91.

Man's main task in life is to give birth to himself, to become what he potentially is. The most important product of his effort is his own personality.[6]

The theologian sees autonomy under God and in relationship to God as the goal of man. Both the psychologist and the theologian agree that an individual must affirm himself, accept himself and direct himself. Each person must be responsible for maintaining a stable set of internal standards by which he acts; have confidence in himself; rely upon his own ability in certain areas of action; develop inner controls that function when needed, and maintain adequate and realistic defenses against threats (or attacks) that come from without.

Very early in life the individual gets an image of himself from the significant people about him. He sees himself as intelligent or stupid, handsome or ugly, second-rate or top-flight. Probably the most important factor in determining how he relates to people is this self-image. He can relate well to other people if he feels that he has a self to present.

A good marriage is a union of two people who feel fairly adequate in giving and receiving. Each must be autonomous.

Dr. Paul Tournier, the Swiss psychiatrist, applies this face-to-face relationship to marriage: "That is what marriage means: helping one another to reach the full status of being persons, responsible and autonomous beings who do not run away from life."[7]

He sees the failure of marriage as precipitated by the running away by the two people from each other and from life. A rich marriage, conversely, is composed of two people who feel good about themselves and who wish to communicate and to remain open to each other. In marriage counseling, the relevance of autonomy is manifold.

In the passive-dominant relationship which we often see—whether the dominant one is the man or the woman—autonomy is involved. The passive one clings to the aggressive mate like a leech. He cannot stand on his own feet and often screams about how he is dominated. The aggressive mate, not being really autonomous, finds

---

[6] Fromm, op. cit., p. 237.

[7] The Meaning Of Persons (New York: Harper & Row, Publishers, 1957), p. 146.

satisfaction in manipulating or leading or nursing the weak one—at the same time losing respect for him.

Of course, if each fully accepts the qualities of the other, even a passive-dominant marriage may be comparatively successful.

Problems of sensitivity are related to autonomy. The less self-containment and self-direction an individual has, the greater his vulnerability. "My feelings get hurt easily" may mean "I have very little autonomy."

The compulsive, driven type of mate finds it hard to respect his mate unless he conforms to the compulsive's ideals. The real identification here is with the pattern or way of life—cleanliness, speech, eating habits, punctuality, etc.—instead of an autonomous affirmation of both the self and the other as unique persons. In other words, the emphasis of such people is on the ritual or pattern instead of on the relationship.

The marriage counselor must try to understand the degree of autonomy each has and the degree of impairment of the individuals in the light of their developmental history. Then he must interpret each to the other. Nothing short of personal therapy will solve the marriage problem if either is too deficient in autonomy.

A third quality in a good marriage is *empathy*. Empathy is the "apprehension of the state of mind of another person without feeling what the other feels. While the empathic process is primarily intellectual, emotion is not precluded, but it is not the same emotion as that of the person with whom one empathizes."[8]

An excellent example of empathy is found in the story of Ezekiel in the Old Testament. Before the prophet could preach to the Hebrews in captivity, he was required to go down by the River Chebar and experience their suffering. "I sat where they sat and remained there astonished [overwhelmed or appalled] among them seven days" (Ezek. 3:15). Ezekiel experienced in some fashion the feelings of these Hebrew captives in their particular set of circumstances. This was empathy. And it was empathy that caused Jesus to weep over Jerusalem's dire condition (Luke 19:41–44).

Empathy is different from sympathy. In sympathy we suffer with the other person. Our suffering may even be more painful to

[8] Horace B. English and Ava Champney English, *A Comprehensive Dictionary of Psychological and Psychoanalytical Terms* (New York: Longmans, Green and Co., 1958).

us than the actual suffering of the other person. Not so with empathy. Empathy involves the projection of oneself into the other person's situation in an attempt to understand what he is feeling.

How can a minister who has never been threatened with divorce understand a man who says that he cannot stand to lose his wife and children? How can he understand a woman who says that she never thought it could happen to her, but she is in love with another man? How can he help a husband see what happened to his wife when she has announced: "I was losing myself so I knew I either had to go to work or go crazy," or a wife who has said: "Every time he touches me I feel dirty"?

The answer to all of these questions is that the minister must draw on his own past emotional experiences and try to reconstruct within himself the other person's feelings.

More important, as he listens to one disturbed mate and then the other, he must learn to record accurately in his own mind what is felt and thought, and try to get some perception of how this situation came to be. Listening is not enough. It is perceiving what is felt and what has happened between these two individuals that is the prime requirement for curing sick marriages.

In the experience of empathy, the counselor maintains a degree of self-awareness and self-control. While he is entering into the others' experiences, he is observing himself feeling and thinking with them. Otherwise he may either remain aloof or over-react. Only by such self-consciousness can the counselor make a creative response to the person or persons who come to him.

Roy Shafer points out the necessity for such empathic understanding in the counseling situation. "An urgent need to cure, to act, to modify does not promote empathic understanding, whereas a reservoir of empathic understanding can effectively guide necessary action, or restraint."[9] This is where many ministers fail in marriage counseling. They tend to superimpose a solution (a verse of Scripture or a prayer) instead of saying to themselves: This person is on a spot; let me see if I can get his predicament well in mind.

Empathy is a necessity, not only for the counseling situation, but for the interpersonal reaction of the couple in trouble, and, for that matter, in any good interpersonal situation.

[9] "Generative Empathy in the Treatment Situation," *The Psychoanalytic Quarterly*, Vol. XXVIII, No. 3, p. 353.

For example, a young man comes home tired and frustrated after a hard day's work. His wife, who has been listening to three children fuss and cry and rebel all day, says: "I want to go out somewhere, anywhere, just to get away from these kids; if I don't I'm going to go crazy." "Go out!" he yells, "I've been out all day— I'm tired. Don't you have any appreciation for what my job is like?" Neither has been able to "enter into" the role of the other. Empathy was absent. Neither heard the other.

Or a man may insist that his wife experience an orgasm every time they have intercourse. As one wife said, "He practically wants a signed affidavit that I have reached a climax." He may feel that he is not a man if he cannot bring about this experience in his wife. She, on the other hand, may be doing her best to "let go," but cannot. If both are empathic to each other, they might find a reasonable adjustment. If not, each may judge the other and attach such labels as "frigid" or "selfish" or "immature" without much perception of what the other is feeling.

No amount of advising or instructing or laying down of rules will solve marriage problems. The function of the marriage counselor is often that of focusing on the importance of understanding. To say: "What does this make her feel?" may be much better than: "You should have known that she would hate you for saying that about her mother."

A fourth aspect of success in marriage is *flexibility*. This may be defined as the ability "to roll with the punches." Changes over which man has little control occur in life. These may be sudden changes in the physical environment, such as automobile accidents, tornadoes, the death of a friend or a sudden attack of physical illness. Or there may be a rapid shift in interpersonal relations, such as betrayal by a friend, the unfaithfulness of a mate, loss of a job by a husband, an unexpected pregnancy or the mental illness of a member of the family.

When these inevitable changes occur, either slowly or suddenly, the individual has to shift gears inside himself. He may have to draw quickly upon his inner resources. He may have to tap new sources of help—God, friends or even counselors. He may have to assume a role that he has never played before.

Doubtless Foote and Cottrell would think of this quality of interpersonal competence as included under the term *autonomy*.

The two are closely related. However, I am thinking here of the ability of an individual to accept hitherto unknown characteristics of a mate as they are brought out by new situations.

Take, for example, a man who was transferred by his company from Kansas City to San Francisco. His wife, reared in Kansas City and with deep emotional and vocational ties there, refused to move. To him this was unreasonable. He thought that a wife should be willing to move wherever her husband's job took him. To her the move was unnecessary. He could make a living in Kansas City if he loved her and was interested in her happiness. The "holy wedlock" became an "unholy deadlock." It ended in divorce.

A woman became infatuated with a neighbor who had shown her excessive attention. The husband found her in the neighbor's arms. Most of their twelve years of married life had been satisfactory, they both said. What was to be done? She admitted that there was no future to her relationship with the neighbor and vowed that she had learned her lesson. Was the husband flexible enough to rebuild a relationship of trust and companionship? Or would he punish and suspect her the rest of her life?

A man, reared in a liberal but religious home, felt that nothing was wrong with keeping a six-pack of beer in the refrigerator. The wife, reared in a conservative faith, said, "I have always said that my children will never see alcoholic beverages in my home." He resented this and thought it stupid. Finally he said, "You can get out, but the beer will come in; this is my home too, you know." She replied, "Right is right and wrong is wrong. If I can't have a Christian home, I don't want one at all."

In another case the husband went out to play poker with his friends while his wife was in the delivery room. "I'll never forget it," she said. "He could, at least, have been there when I came out of delivery; it is his child too."

These are examples of hurt and bitterness that may develop in a marriage. A good part of a successful marriage is the ability to survive such crises and to learn from past mistakes. If the individuals are not resilient, if they have not learned to overcome or transcend traumatic experiences, wounds will not heal and scars will stand out.

The Apostle Paul stated the principle of flexibility clearly, as it concerned his own life, when he said, "I know how to live when things are difficult and I know how to live when things are prosperous. In general and in particular I have learned the secret of facing either poverty or plenty" (Phil. 4:12, Phillips).

Kubie sees the essence of good human adjustment as a specific balance in psychic forces within the personality: "Thus the essence of normality is flexibility, in contrast to the freezing of behavior into patterns of unalterability that characterizes every manifestation of the neurotic process, whether in impulse, purpose, acts, thoughts or feelings."[10] He is saying that normal behavior is reacting to a situation in the light of what is in the situation instead of what is in the subconscious of the individual.

This introduces another element into the problem of interpersonal relations: the subconscious. Whatever our theory of personality structure may be, we must admit that individuals bring from somewhere psychic items that affect their relations with their mates. The man whose wife would not move to California had certain expectations which made him demand that she move with him. The woman who became infatuated may have been looking for an unfulfilled love, which she was not aware of, originally directed toward a father or older brother. The conservative religious woman had definite ideas of a Christian home as she had developed them in an earlier period of her life. And the embittered wife was reacting to her husband, according to her expectations of a husband's role in childbirth.

The situation seems to be this: we may be rigid or inflexible because of numerous influences that have entered our lives from infancy, because of conscious value systems, out of either fear of God or faith in God, out of years of social conditioning or because of feelings that are completely unconscious . . . or all of these together.

Even after the counselor appraises the degree of flexibility in a given relationship, the problem is not solved. It is only diagnosed. His real task is creating a relationship where two people can see the problem and decide on their approach to it—whether to live with it or abandon the relationship or attempt to change. There are no magic keys, either religious or therapeutic, for unlocking rigid people. Many wish to remain as they are; it is often more comfortable.

Of one thing the counselor may be certain: marriages must change. They go through more or less patterned stages. Even the re-

[10] L. S. Kubie, "The Fundamental Nature of the Distinction Between Normality and Neurosis," *Psychoanalytic Quarterly*, Vol. 23 (1954), pp. 187–188.

lationship within a specific period, such as before the first child is born, is in a state of flux.

When a wife says: "Do you think our relationship will ever again be the same?" the best answer may be: "Probably not, but it may be better if both of you wish it to be and will work at it."

This leads to a fifth component of interpersonal competence: *creativity*.

Implicit in this factor in a relationship is hope. Without hope that better ways of relating can be found, neither the counselees nor the counselor has any basis for constructive behavior. This does not mean that every troubled marriage can find a mutually satisfactory way to avoid the divorce court. It takes two hopeful people and a hopeful counselor to find the best working approach to problem marriages.

Creativity means, then, the introduction of the novel into behavior patterns. Foote and Cottrell say the uncreative person is one who "is continually found in dilemmas and impasses—'at his wit's end.'" The creative person is never at loss to find new ways of reacting and is not afraid of diversity, spontaneity, risk-taking and venturesomeness. Creativity follows freedom. It certainly has a degree of freedom as a prerequisite.

The creative person asks: "Did it work?" If it did not, he proceeds to look for alternatives. The rigid and stereotyped person says: "This is the way it ought to be and so I see no reason for changing." The creative person says: "What else shall I try?" whereas the unimaginative person says: "Why try some other way?" Again and again I have found myself saying to someone involved in unsuccessful, repetitive behavior, such as caustic criticism of a mate: "That didn't get anything except bad results, did it?" Sometimes the reply is: "It would if she had sense enough to see it." Again it may be: "I guess that is why we are here, to try to find a better way." There is hope in the latter response.

To depart from the conventional, to think up new patterns of behavior (or new combinations in art) requires courage and risk. Most of us, when faced with a situation that calls for novelty, either look back at the way it has been done, ask someone else how to do it, or think up an alibi for failure. "I can't" is usually an easy way out. To state it differently, we may regress, look away from the problem and simply do the same old things in the same old ways. But the courage to risk failure, to be wrong, to make mistakes is an inherent part of creativity and spontaneity.

Berdyaev writes of creativity as a necessity for overcoming "fettering determinism":

> Creative activity will not come to terms with the given state of the world, it desires another. The creative act always calls up the image of something different; it imagines something higher, better and more beautiful than this—than the "given." . . . The world is full of the results of creative power in the past, which have grown cold and rigid.[11]

In marriages, as well as in society in general, there is this constant need for creativity. A sick marriage is a sure sign that one or both of the couple has not been creative in the relationship.

A twenty-one-year-old wife, with three children, started going to the local dance hall without her husband. She did not drink and at the time I saw her had not become involved with any man. Her twenty-three-year-old husband, a hard worker, could see no reason why she could not be satisfied to sit at home with him in the evenings.

His first move was to threaten to divorce her and take the children away, but a conference with an attorney convinced him that getting the children away from her would be unlikely. His second move was to strike her and attempt to make her feel guilty. His third move was to bring her parents and his into the picture. However, his mother said that he was probably at fault and that he ought to look at himself before he blamed his wife. Her mother joined with the husband in recriminations against her daughter and this led to a somewhat overdue rebellion and defiance on the part of the daughter against her mother.

The turning point came when the husband was able to admit that he had not attempted to meet his wife's social needs. Then, on his own, he asked his wife to teach him to dance, began to take some initiative about their church-going and quit demanding so much of his wife. Slowly their relationship shifted gears.

The wife, in turn, began to see her behavior as immature, looked anew at her relationship to her mother and sought new ways to show her love to her husband.

[11] Nicolas Berdyaev, *The Beginning and the End* (New York: Harper & Row, Publishers, 1952), p. 174.

The crisis resulted in creativity. At church they found other couples their age. He found a lively interest in dancing. As he quit demanding that she get up and fix breakfast for him, she got up of her own accord and fixed him a good breakfast. They found a new way to live together. They established deeper relationships with each other and with others in their community.

Man is most like God when he is creating. We often think of a creator as an artist, a sculptor or a writer. But a man is truly alive when he is creating continuously, in the way he dresses, in conversation with his fellows, in unexpected expressions of affection to his mate and in deviations from the routine or ritualistic patterns of behavior. How can a human being be more significantly creative than in keeping alive the interactions of his family? No marriage need die from boredom if the husband and wife will draw upon their natural resources of creativity.

The application of this to marriage problems is of primary importance because each stage of the marriage calls for new adjustments. Among sociologists, it is a well-known fact that marriages go through stages. Before the first child is born, the mates relate in a particular way. From the time the first child is born until the last one enters school, the husband and wife have distinctive problems. Another phase consists of the period from when the last child enters school until the time that one leaves for college or leaves home. The "empty nest" period sets in when the couple is alone again.

Each of these periods requires creativity. In friendships, in sexual adjustment, in play habits, in religion, in communication, in vocational interests—in all phases of the interpersonal reaction—creativity is essential.

A final component of interpersonal competence is *trust*.

Webster defines trust as "the assured reliance on another's integrity." Erik H. Erikson has said that the infant's first social achievement is his willingness to let the mother out of his sight without giving way to undue anxiety or rage. This is because the child realizes that the mother will continue to act in a predictable pattern: she will return to him. In the process of growth each of us has had both good treatment, as we understood it, and disappointing treatment—these tend to make us creatures of both trust and distrust.

To quote Erikson:

> The general state of trust, furthermore, implies not only that one has learned to rely on the sameness and continuity of the outer providers, but also that one may trust oneself and the capacity of one's own organs to cope with urges; and that one is able to consider oneself trustworthy enough so that the providers will not need to be on guard lest they be nipped.[12]

What Erikson has to say applies to many aspects of interpersonal competence—especially to freedom, autonomy and flexibility. Unless one has a certain degree of trust in another, he would not be outgoing or open to a relationship.

In the counseling relationship and in understanding the interpersonal reactions between a couple, trust is an important component.

In dating, in handling crises in marriage, in rebuilding impaired relationships and in looking to the future of old age together, each must perceive the other as trustworthy and capable of acting in a predictable manner, or a deep relationship will be impossible.

The interpersonal competence approach, as presented here, has attempted to say three things. A good marriage must have, to some degree, these six components. In helping people solve their marriage problems, the successful marriage counselor will need to help the couple deal with their problems in the light of these fundamental aspects. The counseling relationship itself, like all good relationships, will necessarily involve these principles.

[12] *Childhood and Society* (New York: W. W. Norton and Company, Inc., 1950), p. 220.

THREE

The PROBLEM BEHIND
The PROBLEMS

In the following discussion we will look at the utter futility of
the judgmental approach to marital problems and suggest six types
of emotional situations which seem to underlie most surface, presenting problems: (1) the desire to have someone to depend on or
cling to; (2) the need for tenderness or sexual responses within the
marriage; (3) the concept of roles played by husband and wife;
(4) the need to dominate; (5) the dangers of irresponsibility and
insensitivity, and (6) the need for distance and aloofness.

The marriage counselor must ask himself repeatedly: Why have
these two people not been able to achieve some kind of harmony?

The easiest approach to marriage problems is the judgmental
one. We may say that the two people involved are immature. This,
no doubt, will be a true statement. They bring to the marriage ways
of reacting that worked in an earlier period of their lives and which,
they feel, should continue to work. Examples of these may be temper
tantrums, sulking, browbeating, appealing to the other's conscience,
or becoming helpless and sick. But who does not use one of these
childish means of reacting to another at times?

All the term *immaturity* means to some people is that it is a
word useful in condemning behavior patterns that are unpleasant to
them. Inasmuch as human beings do go through various stages in
their development, the term is not without some validity, though it
is often vague and ambiguous. To use *immaturity* as a label for pro-
nouncing moral judgments on others who represent some kind of
threat to us is little better than to return to those labels we had used
on us in childhood, such as *bad, naughty, nasty* or *sinful*. Labels are
easy to come by and probably impossible to avoid. But, they may be
challenged as to their usefulness in changing human behavior.

Neurotic is another label which is in vogue today. As used
popularly, it is simply another way of saying "Thou fool" (to which

Jesus referred). It means: "I don't like you" or "I look down on you" or "Your behavior is objectionable." It is necessary to say what behavior is objectionable and what is approved. Hardly anyone would deny that some behavior is objectionable. But to label a person's behavior as neurotic says very little about what is wrong with it and how it may be changed.

It should be admitted that some labeling of behavior is inevitable in any society. Look at the labels: *righteous—sinful; right—wrong; normal—abnormal; healthy—sick; adjusted—maladjusted; mature—immature.* Each one of these involves some cluster of values, and most of them some authoritarian viewpoint that prescribes a mold or pattern into which we try to fit all people. The plea, here, is that we aim at as clear a definition of terminology as possible and not use terms like *immature, neurotic, abnormal* (these are the popular ones) as clubs with which to hit people over the head.

Suppose the minister thinks in the normal-abnormal framework. Does he think of normality as statistical frequency—*i.e.,* what most people do or say? Most people where? Different societies have different social norms and patterns. In Japan, it is normal to go swimming in the nude. In the inland sections of the United States, among some religious groups, it is a sin to go swimming in a public pool, even in a bathing suit. A few years ago, in this country, the man handled the money, gave his wife an allowance or "grocery money" and made the big decisions himself. Today many women handle the money, pay the bills, and may even give their husbands an allowance. Which is normal or right or ideal?

The marriage counselor, having become wary of fixed labels and of superimposed standards, and with some idea of what makes for interpersonal competence in family life, is confronted with a couple who are having difficulty getting along. From the very first, he must be alert to the personalities of these two people. Adjustment problems cannot be solved apart from the personality structure of the persons involved. Another way of saying this is that all marriage problems are emotional problems. If we deal merely with the presenting problem, with the "symptoms" (to use the physician's term), we will not get at the cause of the problem. It would be like a physician who gives a sedative for sleeplessness or anodyne for a headache.

What, then, are the major problems which lie behind the presenting problem? It would be fairly easy to find out from current sociological studies that most marriage problems center around money, sex, in-laws, discipline of children, etc. But why cannot these two people solve these problems? Others do. What is wrong with these two people that they cannot find some working approach to their money or sex or in-law problems?

Another way of thinking of marriage problems, for any counselor, is this: What are we to look for so far as the real problem is concerned? As Laurence S. Kubie, M.D., has pointed out: "Men and women are infinitely ingenious in their ability to find new ways of being unhappy together; so that even with unlimited space it would be impossible to illustrate every variety of marital misery."[1]

We shall begin with a type of problem that, from my experience, is the most common one: the desire to have someone to depend on or cling to.   One writer on marriage problems says: "I am convinced the frailty that renders us so vulnerable to the misfortunes that develop in marriage is the tendency to retain our early passive, receptive and dependent nature."[2] He refers to these as the "early" traits because we come into this world utterly dependent and spend a long period of our earthly existence wholly or partly dependent on someone else—no other creature has such a lengthy dependency period.

No one will deny that a child needs to be loved and cared for, even catered to, by adults. But when an individual enters a marriage believing that he has the divine right to be loved no matter how he behaves, he is headed for trouble. Even if he behaves well, he will not be loved as much as he wishes to be. Most human beings are not loved as they secretly wish to be. Their only alternative is to love and respect themselves and to act in a manner that will get reasonable love and respect from others.

John B. married Sarah B. as soon as he returned from the service, which he had entered after being graduated from high school. Sarah had expressed misgivings about entering the marriage at the time, but John had threatened suicide if she did not marry him. For six years now she has managed his money, talked him out of quitting

[1] "Psychoanalysis and Marriage: Practical and Theoretical Issues," in *Neurotic Interaction in Marriage*, edited by Victor W. Eisenstein (New York: Basic Books, Inc., 1956), p. 15.

[2] Harry F. Tashman, *The Marriage Bed* (New York: University Publisher, Inc., 1959), p. 301.

his job, bought his clothes for him and maneuvered him into going to church.

Even though he held a very good job, he was highly competitive with Sarah, complaining bitterly if she worked overtime at her job and insinuating that she must have a crush on someone at her office. If she could not respond to him sexually when she was tired, he frequently turned over in bed and cried himself to sleep.

When she finally moved out of their house into an apartment, he proceeded to run to all the relatives and to urge them to talk some sense into her head, professed deep and profound love for her, threatened to let her dog starve, asked to move in with her if she would not come back to the house and frequently had crying spells in front of her if she talked of divorce. The more he told her of his love and how much he needed her, the less she saw him as a man. His final move, another threat of suicide, brought her to a firm decision to get a divorce. He is now in therapy trying to face his dependency needs, so that he will not repeat his past mistakes.

Sarah admitted that John was a hard worker, an honest and good man, but she did not love him. She wanted a "man" as a husband. In counseling she was able to see that she had contributed to his dependency, that she had felt sorry for him when she had married him and that her need to mother him had grown out of her own feelings of inadequacy as a self-respecting, desirable female.

If they had looked for help in the first years of marriage, there might have been hope for this marriage. John might have learned to stand on his own feet, and Sarah might have been able to respect him and build an adult relationship with him.

Extreme dependency and lack of autonomy often manifest themselves in problems of extreme competition with in-laws or friends, excessive sexual demands, drinking as an escape from loneliness, revengeful love affairs or sexual episodes and quarrels over small matters that obscure the real issues. The real issue with a dependent person is this: "You do not love me and cater to me as I wish to be loved and catered to."

A more subtle type of passive-dependent person is that of the mate who wishes to be loved but refuses to attempt to give love. In sexual relations this type complains bitterly that he has to make all the advances. Or the wife may rationalize that she thinks it is the husband's place to make all of the advances. Usually such people cannot make clean-cut decisions, constantly feel sorry for themselves and may even develop physical illnesses as a means of getting cared for.

A second problem which confronts the pastor is that of tenderness or sexual responses within the marriage.   There is much misinformation about sex. These range all the way from the belief that masturbation will cause one to be a bad marriage partner to the theory that unless a woman reaches an orgasm during intercourse she will not become pregnant. Among fairly well-educated people, one often finds such misconceptions as the belief that sexual intercourse during the woman's menstrual period will cause damage to the female genital; or that there is no chance of pregnancy if the man puts on a contraceptive just before he ejaculates, or that the "safe" period is midway between the woman's menstrual periods.

Some books and magazine articles have led people to believe that unless a woman achieves a climax in a certain manner she will be nervous and unhappy and is abnormal. Another misconception is that a man who has frequent sex relations will incur prostate gland trouble.

These misconceptions can be removed only by a better presentation of facts. Physicians often do a good job of presenting these facts if their patients will reveal to them the areas where they have intellectual blind spots. The minister, however, cannot depend on the counselee's getting the facts either from physicians or books.

The minister should keep constantly in mind that most so-called sexual difficulties in marriage are not primarily of sexual origin.

Erich Fromm points out that it is a fallacy to assume "that the real problem between the sexes is sex" and that the great stimuli for sex are often vanity, loneliness and the drive to prove oneself superior.

Kubie holds a similar view, as shown by the following quotation: "I have never seen a marriage made or broken by sex alone, except in the case of frank perversions."[3] He points out that many people are so laden with deep-seated feelings of sexual guilt that they can tolerate sex only as long as it is unsuccessful, and consequently react to an orgasm with guilt or panic. His point is that what seems to be a perfectly normal sexual response might leave some people in a state

[3] L. S. Kubie, "Husband-Wife," *The People in Your Life,* edited by Margaret M. Hughes (New York: Alfred Knopf, 1951), p. 50.

of rage or panic or depression because of their basically unwholesome attitude toward pleasure and happiness.

Such insights show the futility of sex education which stresses physiology and anatomy. Sex is no better and no worse than the total relationship of the people involved. For the marriage counselor, this means that the complaints about sexual inadequacies on the part of one mate must be correlated with the preconceptions of the individual who is complaining. What did he expect of the mate sexually? What other emotions, such as resentment, self-pity and fear of failure, may be entering into the picture? Does one mate feel "used" in the sexual act? Is one actually stronger than the other sexually? Or is this a case of one's not knowing how to evoke the love response of the other? How does the tenderness response correlate with other responses such as verbal communication, working for common goals and the self-fulfillment in recreation and religion?

A third problem that enters into many marriage difficulties is the concept of roles played by husband and wife. "In my father's family a man made the living and the woman did the housework and attended to the children. My wife thinks that she can wear the pants and I'm not about to let that happen. No woman is going to henpeck me. If my wife wants to work, she had just as well make up her mind that she can get her housework done the best she can."

These were the words of a twenty-nine-year-old man who felt that his wife, a bookkeeper, was about to get the better of him. He went fishing with the boys when he wished, cashed his wife's check, paid the bills and gave his wife the allowance he thought she ought to have. What was she unhappy about? It is true that their sexual life had gone to pot. The girls at work kidded her about her husband walking all over her and not giving her any extra money. Her mother bought clothes for her and the children. Her husband would not attend church with her, but insisted that she and the children go. Now that she had become more and more nervous, she saw no way out but divorce. What was destroying this marriage?

The husband had entered the marriage with one idea of the husband-wife relationship, and she with another. Her mother had been the dominant one in her family, and she had vowed she would never be like her, so she married a man who would not allow her to henpeck him. Secretly she had admired his strength and forceful-

ness. Inwardly, also, she had resented him for his overbearing manner. It was hardly possible for her to hold her job and do all of the
housework. She hated housework anyway. Her mother had worked
out of the home, and her father had helped with the housework.
Why could her husband not be as helpful?

This confused picture is not uncommon in our day of the changing role of the male and female. Here the husband was patterning
his marriage after that of his parents. He married a wife who pre-
ferred working to being a housewife, yet felt the need to do both.
He was stronger than her father, which she liked, but he did not
have the cooperative attitudes her father had. Soon she became torn
between being a person in her own right; being a mother and a
housewife, and being a "good" wife. When the triple role became
too great, she resolved the issue by getting out of the marriage and
assuming only two roles: that of mother and career person. It seemed
simpler to her.

As a result of the marriage failure, the husband became an ab-
sentee breadwinner, paying child support and looking for another
mate who would make him feel like a man.

In our era of the changing roles of the husband and wife, some
crucial problems arise in the home. They may be centered around
the following questions: Who handles the money and pays the bills?
Who makes the sexual advances? Who disciplines the children?
Who is the final authority in making major decisions? Who does the
buying of groceries and other regular necessities?

The pastor will see all sorts of variations in how men and
women perceive their roles. He will do well to try to clarify these
issues, helping each mate to perceive the other's view of the situation,
rather than to approach the problem from an *ex cathedra* position of
what the roles ought to be.

*A fourth hidden problem which lies behind many mar-
riage difficulties is the need to dominate on the part of one
or both of the mates.* This is a very subtle emotional need and
one that involves a great deal of face-losing on the part of the counselee. Some simply cannot admit this need. In such cases the marriage
will be dissolved, or the dominated one will have to accept the manipulative aspect of the other or conflict will be a constant part of the
marriage. Sometimes, however, the manipulative one will be able to

face himself and change the relationship into one of freedom and mutuality.

Basically, the need to dominate grows out of insecurity. Its origins may be in the child's natural desire to have things his own way, the concept of role differentiation, the fear of having "the rug jerked out from under him" (which must be understood in the light of the developmental history of the individual) or the lack of respect for the autonomy of other individuals. The kind of security which every individual seeks, especially in a marriage, is "a feeling that one enjoys the respect of the other person in a situation and that one respects oneself."[4] Anything that lowers an individual's self-esteem will cause him anxiety and arouse him to some kind of unfavorable response.

The manipulative response may express itself in a thousand different ways in the marriage relationship. The focus of the problem may be on which relatives to visit at Christmas; whether to buy a motor boat or a new suite of furniture; when to spank the child; how often to attend church; how many drinks are "too many"; whether to take out an insurance policy; whether to accept a proffered gift from the grandparents; how often to have sexual relations; whether the wife should prepare breakfast for the husband; whether the husband should accept a promotion which requires a move to another city, or who is going to say grace at the table.

In such cases the counselor may be tempted to tell one that he is wrong or to say: "My wife and I do so-and-so," but neither of these approaches will be effective. Each marriage structure is different. The counselor's greatest opportunity lies in assisting each to understand how the other feels, asking them to come up with alternative solutions and confronting the more manipulative one with the reasons (in the light of his own background) for his need to "call the shots." If the need of one to control is too great for the other to tolerate, and if the "controller" is motivated to change, a prolonged period of counseling is indicated. In which case, if a change in behavior occurs, the dominated one will probably need some counseling also, inasmuch as he will have to "shift gears" when the change occurs.

An example of the need to "shift gears" is that of a woman who

[4] Patrick Mullahy, "The Theories of H. S. Sullivan," *The Contributions of Harry Stack Sullivan* edited by Patrick Mullahy (New York: Hermitage House, 1952), pp. 23–24.

had related to a very passive man as a controller and a dominating mate. As he changed she experienced some anxiety and sent me the following telegram from another city (they moved before the transition was fully established): "You convinced Jimmy of autonomy and individuality. I liked him better henpecked. Please refrain from future encouragement. However, I will remain devotedly your follower." The touch of humor in this telegram is probably the saving factor in this marriage. She needed to dominate, but she was objective enough about her needs to be able to accept the confrontation without too much loss of self-esteem.

A fifth reaction pattern that enters into sick marriages is that of **irresponsibility and insensitivity** *on the part of one of the mates.*   Irresponsible and insensitive people are the most hopeless types of marriage mates. They are one of the types who get involved in from four to ten different marriages and are sometimes extremely hard to spot.

On the surface these people appear very genial, sincere, open, frank and convincing. Their primary characteristics are that they do not conform to the rules of society; do not care deeply for anyone; relate superficially and often charmingly to most people; rationalize easily about why they behave as they do, and take great pride in their ability to con their way in and out of any situation. There are all degrees of impairment, of course, in these people. Some act out (do as they please at the moment) in drink, sex, writing bad checks, speeding, refusing to work, fits of anger and violence, lying and even pretending to go through genuine religious conversions. Others act out only in refusing to seek employment and in, say, anger and lying.

Intellectually, these people know all the answers but do not apply them to themselves. They even know that their behavior will not work, that their chance of getting into trouble is very great. Not infrequently they will have worked out astute analyses as to why they are as they are. It is not uncommon for them if they are in a difficult situation (such as threatened arrest or divorce) to make apparently sincere resolutions to "straighten up and fly right," promising never to do again what they have done in the past. Depending on the degree of impairment, they may flagrantly act out again within the next twenty-four hours. They know better but seem not to find the resources, either within themselves or from God, to change their behavior.

Emotionally such people are flat, never feeling deeply about anyone. If they cry, the counselor can be pretty sure that they are crocodile tears, designed to get results in convincing someone else to change. Their utter insensitivity to the needs and requirements of other people make them unable to relate richly to anyone. They do not experience empathy, and they lack autonomy.

The minister is faced with three very pertinent facts, even if he sees very clearly the type of person with whom he is dealing. First, the mate who marries the irresponsible person almost invariably has a need to be hurt and will find it difficult to face this fact or to give up the relationship, however intolerable. Second, the general public finds it hard to believe that such people really exist or that no one, including the religionist, has found a way of helping such people change. Third, referring the irresponsible person to a psychiatrist will do no good (even if the psychiatrist will accept him in therapy), because he will usually go only three or four times for therapy; and, as a rule, such a person cannot be hospitalized in a mental hospital under present existing laws and customs.

This type of marriage choice will be dealt with further in the chapter on "Which Cases Are Hopeless." Note here should be made of an observation by Ackerman:

> Character disorders do not exist alone; they function in pairs and threesomes. For every person suffering from a character disorder there are one or more partners who share in the problem.[5]

A sixth type of personality problem which the pastor sees is found in those people who have a need for distance and aloofness. This may exist in one or both mates. If in both, they may find a relationship that will be tolerable, if both can see what the situation is. If one is very much in need of closeness or warmth, the marriage may become intolerable.

The aloof person, of the type here indicated, complains loudly of his rejection by his mate. He may say that she is being unfaithful to him, that she thinks more of her mother than of him, that she is cold sexually or that she is incapable of love. "I never felt that she loved me and the more I tried to gain her respect and love, the more

[5] Nathan W. Ackerman, "The Psychoanalytic Approach to the Family," *Individual and Familial Dynamics,* edited by Jules H. Masserman (New York: Grune and Stratton, 1959), p. 113.

she withdrew from me," he may say. The wife may report that from the first he was tight with his money, critical of her housekeeping, unable to relate to their friends and arrogant and opinionated when they tried to discuss anything. If she was friendly with another man, he would say, "What the hell do you see in that jerk?" If she tried to get him interested in recreation, his reply was that he wasn't a child any more and wasn't about to waste his life playing some silly games.

In counseling he may barely be able to admit that he had been too serious all of his life, that he had some kind of need to keep people away from him and that his marital problem may have been partly his fault. He might not be able to see that the rejection by his wife was something that he had brought about himself, by his own behavior, or that he could not stand for people to get close to him lest they find out how empty or unlovable he was.

In one case the wife gained enough insight into her husband's personality and had enough self-containment of her own to live in a "limited marriage" while he largely went his way and she her way. As each shifted out of the judgmental approach, the relationship became more livable.

There are numerous other types of problem types, such as the over-independent who never really marries emotionally; the hungry person who sees tenderness as a weakness and, therefore, starves, or the obsessive-compulsive person who is really married to his job and to achievement, although he feels the need for closeness in marriage. The above, however, illustrate the fact that the focus on what people fight about, or what they are unhappy about, will not change the marriage difficulties. It is the personality problems behind the presenting conflict situations that must be faced.

FOUR

The INITIAL INTERVIEW

When a couple walk into a minister's study, the minister is faced with the immediate problem of getting started in finding out the difficulty. He may know only their names, or that they attend church and live at a certain address. If they are strangers to him, such as those who are not members of his church, he will wish to get well in mind such matters as their names; their addresses; whether or not they go to church and where, and how they happened to come to him. If they are much younger than himself, he will need to get their first names accurately and perhaps their familiar names, such as "Jack" for John or "Pat" for Patricia.

If there is a relaxed, unhurried, warm attitude on the part of the pastor, sometimes all that is needed to get the ball rolling is an alert, wide-awake smile directed toward them after they are comfortably seated. A "dead pan" or disinterested look will create the worst possible atmosphere for counseling. If the pastor arranges the two chairs side by side so he can observe both and seats himself in a comfortable manner, usually all he will need to say is: "Tell me about your problem."

It is my opinion that under no circumstances should the counselor talk across a desk to individuals. It creates the impression of aloofness and a stereotyped business relationship rather than one of friendliness and communication between equals. Anything that avoids the here-I-sit-with-all-the-answers pose will be an asset. If a desk is the necessary furniture for the counseling room and the pastor has to use the chair behind the desk, the next best arrangement is to talk with the counselees across the corner of the desk.

As the interview proceeds, the pastor will pick up pertinent basic facts about the two, even if direct questions must be interjected. If it seems necessary, the pastor may say, "Pardon me for interrupting at this point, but let me get some facts in mind." Then he may simply ask how long they have been married, how many children there are, their ages and sex, how long they went together before marriage, what the husband does for a living, if the wife works and anything else that is not too personal and which may seem important.

GETTING STARTED ON THE PROBLEM

The pastor need not be entirely passive as a listener in the first or any other interview. People do not understand a relationship where one just sits and stares. If the counselee says something which is puzzling, startling, shocking, alarming or funny, there is no good reason why the pastor should not react like any other normal human being. The most significant aspect of a first interview, however, is to get the "feel" of what the individuals are saying and to let them know that you got it. This may be done by the well-known method of reflecting the feeling of the counselee.

Wife: I told him that if his mother was going to stay in our house she was going to have to stop criticizing me. But he said that it was his mother's and his house and he would have whom he damned pleased in it.

Pastor: This made you feel that you were an outsider and didn't amount to anything in that household?

Husband: Now, pastor, that is not exactly the way it happened. My mother had not visited us for a year, not since Dad died, and I felt that we ought to have her to come. What I told Joyce was that it was my house and I did not see any reason why my mother could not come to see us. I was mad. Maybe I did say more than I should have, but Mother is old. I know Mother is bossy and critical. I know that, but Joyce is going to have to learn not to be so sensitive.

Pastor: Let me see if I get this straight. You felt some obligation to your mother—maybe you felt sorry for her—and Joyce's resistance made you feel that she didn't have any understanding of your mother's needs.

Husband: Yes, I think Joyce is selfish and too sensitive.

Wife: But what about her criticizing my cooking and the way

I kept my house? I guess you think I ought to just sit there and let her criticize me. Not on your life!

Pastor: Wait a minute. All you are doing at this point is blaming each other. I don't get this. It seems to me that each of you fails to put himself in the other's shoes.

Up until the last remarks the pastor was trying to reflect and clarify the feelings of the counselees. Then he confronted them with the futility of the way they were approaching the problem, and pointed toward the importance of empathy. Note that the pastor bypassed the "my house" attitude of the husband and the more threatening content of the labels that he was applying to Joyce—"selfish" and "sensitive." He could have jumped at the absurdity of the "my house" attitude. Instead, his first task was to see precisely what these two people were feeling, how they handled a critical situation and how capable they were of accepting insights into interpersonal difficulties.

In marriage problems it seems that there is value in seeing the two together at first. Not only does the counselor get some idea of how they interact, but each has an equal start in revealing the facts as he sees them.

During the first interview the pastor may say, "I would like to talk with each of you alone. Later we will talk together. Mr. ———, will you wait in the outer office until I call you?"

In these separate interviews more intimate details may be explored and, usually, each will have more personal viewpoints to express.

Counselee: I didn't want to say this before him, but I have a letter here, which he doesn't know that I have, from the woman in Hawaii. He says nothing happened between them, but the woman says she is pregnant and talks about the pleasure they had together. Do you want to read it?

Pastor: If you wish me to [takes letter and reads it].

Counselee: This is confidential, isn't it? You will not tell him that I have the letter?

Pastor: Of course not. I not only will not tell him, but a pastor is under the law of "privileged communication." They cannot make me tell what is told me in confidence, even in court.

QUESTIONS THAT BRING OUT
THE BASIC DIFFERENCES

Many people come to the pastor with a very vague notion of what the real problems are in their marriage. Dean Johnson states the distinctive nature of the first interview very succinctly:

> The initial interview is controlled and directed by the counselor. It is controlled because the interviewer needs to get the essential facts involved in the client's situation as quickly as possible. He also needs to evaluate the client's motivation in seeking help. . . . If by being passive, the counselor allows the client to talk without direction, and thus fails to guide the interview, the client may anticipate that by pouring out his difficulties, he will be able to shift the burden of them onto the counselor, who will then arrive at solutions for him.[1]

When I hear pastors say, "I just listened to them," I cannot but wonder what kind of impression this left on the counselees. They may have thought "What kind of a dumb bunny is this who does not have a viewpoint of his own and who would not even act surprised when I told him about slapping my wife?"

In the initial interview the pastor may discover the cause of the marital unhappiness by asking certain pertinent questions. It is not suggested that all of these questions will be used in every initial interview or in any particular order, but that the kinds of information and responses which these questions evoke may be of value in evaluating what routes to take in helping the couple to find their solutions:

> What do you fight about?
> When did this marriage start downhill?
> What was the dating and courtship period like?
> What was the marriage like before that?
> What is good in the marriage?
> How do you see your sexual adjustment?
> What do you think makes him (or her) like this?
> How do you differ?
> Have you often talked of divorce?
> Why did you marry him?

[1] *Marriage Counseling: Theory and Practice* (Englewood Cliffs, N.J.: Prentice-Hall, Inc., 1961), pp. 61–62.

Such questions as these, kept in mind and used when it seems natural to use them, may get at the facts of the marital problem without the formal "taking of the case history."

If minimal factual material is needed, a blank form, such as the one suggested in Chapter Ten, may be used, in which case the pastor's secretary may have one for the couple to fill out when they arrive for the interview. If a secretary is not available, the pastor may ask them to take a moment to fill it out before he sees them.

DEMONSTRATING THE
COUNSELING APPROACH

Counseling starts from the moment the couple enters the counseling room. Everything should be focused on the counselees. Note-taking or fact-gathering should become secondary, or be entirely removed, if they detract in any way from the personal encounter between the counselor and the counselees. Communication, verbal and nonverbal, goes on all the time. If a counselee drums on the chair with his fingers, flicks one fingernail against the other, swings one leg backwards and forwards, slouches in the chair or pulls her dress down well over her knees, the alert counselor will observe this in silence. If tears come to the eyes as certain subjects are dealt with, note must be made as to the meaning of this intensity. We can recall the wisdom of a popular song of a few years ago reminding us that every little movement has a meaning of its own.

The initial interview may make or break the whole process of counseling. This need not create anxiety for the counselor. He must be himself and respond as he can within his framework of sincerity and helpfulness. His primary role is not that of a savior but that of a friend—a friend who does not profess to have the answers, but who will look at the problems through the counselee's eyes and try to point out what he sees or does not see.

Inasmuch as most people haven't the faintest idea what to expect from a counselor, they can only learn what counseling is like by entering into it. A first interview cannot be a typical interview because the picture must be seen before the problems can be attacked. It can have in common with all other subsequent interviews the factors of perceiving what the counselees are feeling, showing

respect for their present state and for them in this state and display-
ing confidence that they will be able to find solutions.

It is not do's and don't's that are needed by the counselor. What
he does or does not do must grow out of a basic attitude that the
solutions he has found for himself may not be the ones that these
two people may find. It is an attitude of respect for the uniqueness of
each life and of the uniqueness of each human situation. Moreover,
for him to try to superimpose his own viewpoint or even what he
believes to be God's viewpoint is little short of playing God.

Ackerman and Behrens, writing of what they call "therapeutic
intervention"—in dealing with other members of the family while
trying to help the troubled one—have a frank and interesting com-
ment about "playing God":

> Every therapist plays God a little bit. And some "gods" make
> mistakes. We wonder, too, if it is playing God any less to attempt
> to cure individuals of their emotional suffering, while isolating the
> individual and doing nothing about his family environment. As in
> the case with every job in life, when one plays God, one must know
> what one is doing.[2]

Although they are dealing here with the question of whether to
treat more than one member of a family at a time, at least in a supportive way, their point is well taken if applied to most counseling
situations. For the minister, however, since he is already cast in the
God-role, there is a need for a word of caution. If he assumes an
authoritative and manipulative role, he will likely find himself assuming responsibilities which, according to the minister's own theology and according to the hard facts of life, belong inherently to
each person as he stands on his own feet "before God."

PLANNING THE COUNSELING PROGRAM

Pastor: Now that you have told me something of your problems, I am sure you know that you have been years getting this way. Perhaps even some of your problems

2 Nathan W. Ackerman and Marjorie L. Behrens, "The Family Group and
Family Therapy: The Practical Application of Family Diagnosis," in *Prog-
ress in Psychotherapy*, edited by Jules H. Masserman and J. L. Moreno (New
York: Grune and Stratton, 1958), p. 65.

started long before marriage. It may be of value at this point to try to put into words exactly what you feel I can do to help you.

Wife: Well, I figured that you would tell us what we could do. This fighting is getting us nowhere. What do you think we ought to do?

Husband: Yeah, we didn't know where to turn. Sally said that you had helped others she knew about, and I figured if you could help us it would be worth a try.

Pastor: I appreciate your confidence more than I can tell you. But I wonder if you two realize how slow and painful counseling can be.

Wife: We don't want to cause you any trouble, Pastor. We know how busy you are.

Pastor: Oh, I didn't mean painful to me. I meant that if you two are going to solve your problems and find a good working relation to each other, it is going to require you to look at yourselves. What you are going to see, in some instances, is not going to be very pleasant. (Pause) I will be very glad to try to help you if you will realize that I am not a magician and that most of what is done will be done by you.

Husband: What do you want us to do in the meantime?

Pastor: Just try to look at yourselves and talk to each other. I don't know what you *can* or *will* be able to do. When you come in, just try to be frank about yourselves. Are there any questions?

Wife: Just one thing. Pastor, do you think this marriage will ever work?

Pastor: I think so. It will depend largely on you two. You certainly have a lot at stake. We don't even know yet, or at least I do not, why it hasn't worked. Let's try to understand that first. It takes patience to unlearn habit patterns that have been with you, some of them for years. It's like going to a doctor and finding out that you have a disease that takes more than one shot to cure. Do you want to come in next week?

Husband: I'm going to be out of town all next week. Why can't you see Sally next week and let me come in the next?

Pastor: All right. In the meantime, let's see what you can do on your own. Work at it.

Here the pastor assumed both his fatherly role by gently encouraging the couple to work at the marriage and his counseling role by simply promising to talk the problems out with them. The two are not in conflict. Indeed, they may augment each other. As counselor he has arranged the subsequent interviews and structured the relationship so they do not see him as a god who can solve their problems without any effort on their part. If they should not come back, he has, at least, dealt with the matter in a straightforward and realistic manner.

FOR THOSE WHO WANT "FIRST AID"

Many people turn to the various helping professions merely to get a little help. They want "first aid." Having gotten that, they go right on living with their problems and never find a very satisfactory approach. Their initial interview becomes their last one, at least for awhile.

It may be because they come to realize that the solution will require more time and patience than they wish to give. Sometimes one may not be able to relate to the counselor—this need not be a reflection on either. Some feel much better after they have sat down and told their story, and decide that they might as well "let well enough alone." Others actually make considerable changes rather quickly and get the feel of a good relationship, and from here move on in life.

It is sometimes disappointing to see people live second-rate lives in a very limited marriage. One may even be tempted to condemn such people as vain or self-righteous. The pastor-counselor helps people as they wish to be helped when they are open for help.

THOSE WHO NEED SEPARATE COUNSELORS

It should be recognized that some types of counselees need to see a separate counselor from the one the mate is seeing. This is for the very simple reason that the counseling relationship is one of confidence and mutuality and is often disturbed if another member of the family is in the picture. Such a relationship has to be carefully built. Some would claim that this is not marriage counseling, thereby restricting marriage counseling to dealing with interpersonal relations—perhaps superficially—rather than with the individual's personality quirks that may be the heart of the marriage problem. It is my feeling that marriage counseling cannot be separated from personal counseling and psychotherapy. One verges into the other as naturally as an infection in one part of the body may affect the functioning of the whole person.

Most pastors will either deal as competently as they can with the marriage problems which come to them, or they will refer the couple to some other professional counselor. If a pastor is to undertake their counseling, he will usually see each one on alternate weeks, or both at the same hour each week (sometimes twice a week), with the session split about equally between them. In many cases he will see regularly the one who is most disturbed, and will see the other in a kind of supportive-guidance interview every few weeks. This last, however, may lead to rivalry, with the result that the one seen most often may come to feel that "the monkey is on his back" while the one seldom seen may come to feel neglected.

There is no rule of thumb for when and whom and how often to see counselees in marriage counseling. The personality of the counselor and the maturity of the counselees must determine these details. Two things can be said: (1) Try not to get caught in the middle of the marital conflict with one or both feeling that you are taking sides. (2) Don't spend hours at one time talking with the couple. Experience has proved that this is not profitable. Limit the time and set a subsequent time for further discussion.

Those who see people in marriage counseling find that most of them fall into four categories: (1) marriages in which one needs a great deal of help and the other needs some supportive help while, and if, the most needy one changes; (2) marriages in which each needs some help and, while changes are occurring, the interpersonal picture will need to be understood by both; (3) marriages in which both need to work at a better interpersonal relationship without much tampering with the individuals as such; (4) marriages in which both are seriously impaired and need prolonged help in order to relate well to each other or to anyone else.

In the last type of problem, referral of one or both to another counselor is highly desirable, if such help is available and can be afforded. However, such help is not available in many parts of the United States, either in public clinics or from private practitioners. The time will probably come when two pastors with adjoining parishes will collaborate in referring one of the disturbed mates to the other pastor. Then, at the proper time, the four will sit down together to review the progress to date and to determine the future procedures.

In the first three categories of marriage (mentioned above), the pastor, because of his role, may be in a particularly good position to help. If he can say to the husband, for example: "It seems that your wife is the one who is most upset at this point. If she and I can talk for a few sessions to see if we can get a better understanding of the problem, it may be of value. This does not mean, of course, that she is more at fault or that she is sick mentally, only that she needs to see herself better before she can attack the problem. I hope you will stand by, or call me anytime you wish, until she and I get further along in seeing what the trouble is."

In the second and third categories, perhaps equal time will be spent with both the husband and wife. This may be done in a split-session of thirty minutes each or by rotation of appointments on alternate weeks.

The trend in the field of family counseling is toward "whole family" counseling. While individuals are seen in individual counseling, it may be of increasing value to sit down with all the involved adults in the family—and even the teen-agers—in the attempt to help each to see the other's viewpoint as they interact. At least, the pastor should be constantly alert to the fact that if one member of a family "grows up," changes, it is of primary importance that the other members understand what is happening and make necessary adjustments. Otherwise, the individual may be saved but the marriage wrecked.

In the initial interview, the stage is set for immediate future counseling, for referral or for subsequent help, sometimes months later. It requires tact, patience and confidence to play it by ear and to be as helpful as possible in relating to two people who obviously have a problem but may not understand how they can be helped or by whom.

FIVE

FINDING A WORKING APPROACH

Philip Wagner, in discussing the way the great psychiatrist, the late Dr. Harry Stack Sullivan, approached human problems, says:

> Despite his dourness there was an optimism based on conviction that no matter how great the mess there was always a way out, even if the way out was not evident to the therapist. He urged his students never to let a patient go with the final conviction within them that things were hopeless and nothing could be done. One could not imagine Sullivan saying to a patient, 'Well, we have had a trial analysis and psychoanalysis cannot be of use to you. Good-bye."[1]

This basic optimism, grounded in the faith that God is working in each of our lives to show his "transcendent power," led the Apostle Paul into a flight of eloquence in his second letter to the Corinthian Church:

> We are afflicted in every way, but not crushed; perplexed, but not driven to despair; persecuted, but not forsaken; struck down, but not destroyed (2 Cor. 5: 8–9).

In a marriage relationship, the aim is a self-in-relationship-with-the-other. It is a security-in-relationship, not in isolation. In order to solve marriage problems we must look at (1) what goes on inside the individual; (2) what goes on between this person and others, and (3) the interpersonal patterns which characterize the group of which the individual is a part.[2]

With the above framework in mind—optimism concerning the

[1] *The Contributions of Harry Stack Sullivan*, ed. Patrick Mullahy (New York: Hermitage House, 1952), p. 157.
[2] Nathan W. Ackerman and Marjorie L. Behrens, "The Family Group and Family Therapy: The Practical Application of Family Diagnosis," *Progress in Psychotherapy*, Vol. III, edited by Jules H. Masserman and J. L. Moreno (New York: Grune and Stratton, 1958), p. 67.

individual, an awareness of his interpersonal complex relationships and perception of how the culture impinges on his thinking, feeling and action—we may now face some of the specific marriage problems that confront the pastor. These, again, do not exhaust the various possibilities but are typical of the problems the pastor is presented with.

This discussion follows the consideration of the initial interview because it is often only in the second or third interview that such problems become apparent. It precedes the discussion of the working through of cases because often two or three sessions is as far as some couples wish to go. Many people do not wish to remove their neurotic patterns, nor to find the most mature way of handling their problems, and certainly not to understand how the pattern of behavior relates to cultural influences. They merely wish to find some kind of working approach to prevent the complete dissolution of the marriage. The marriage counselor need not disdain such limited motivation.

SEXUAL DIFFICULTIES

What for example, is the best approach to the problems of a husband who says, "My wife does not seem interested in sex as often as I am"? He might undergo psychoanalysis and discover that he was seeking assurance for himself from his wife through the sexual act and that the need for such reassurance grew out of a feeling of competition with his father. His wife might undergo analysis and discover that her disinterest in sex grew out of a deep resentment of men and her own rejection of herself for not having a penis. Most probably, however, neither will submit to analysis.

The working approach must involve such matters as finding out what each really expects of the other; how they came to form their opinions about how frequently sex should be enjoyed, and the emotional factors that may be clouding the picture. From there must come the development of good communication patterns and a willingness to experiment with new ways of responding to each other.

It has already been pointed out that sexual problems, as a rule, are problems not of sex but of interpersonal relations problems and emotional problems (see Chapter Three). With this in mind, let us look at some types of sexual maladjustments that are involved in marital unhappiness.

Most sexual difficulties fall into four categories: (1) lack of agreement on the frequency of intercourse; (2) inability to respond according to one's own or one's mate's concept of what sex ought to be; (3) desire for sexual behavior which, for some reason, seems abnormal to the mate, and (4) involvement by one mate in an extramarital relationship which is intolerable to the other mate. Let us look at each of these in terms of what immediate working approach may be found to the problem.

The first problem is lack of agreement on frequency of intercourse. Our first attack on this problem is to discover what each expects from the other and how they arrived at their conclusions. From published literature, from conversations with friends or from instruction from authoritative sources (church, parents, or even doctors), one of the mates may have drawn the conclusions that sex should be enjoyed only occasionally. One may be more desirous of sex than the other, for reasons which are not readily observable. Two normal people are capable of a variety of patterns. The problem here consists of removing preconceived notions and substituting for them realistic ideas that will be reasonably satisfying to both.

In the second category, the problems are more complex. One mate may not be able to respond fully—and "fully" can mean almost anything. A husband may not be able to get an erection. The wife may not be able to reach an orgasm. The husband may not know how to carry out the love play which precedes intercourse as the wife understands such play should be carried on. Or, the husband may think the wife too passive and not as enthusiastic as she should be in the sexual embrace. He may believe that unless a wife experiences an orgasm she gets no satisfaction from intercourse. She may think that unless he reaches a climax in a given length of time (some books say from three to five minutes) he has been masturbating or indulging in another sexual outlet. He or she may feel that something is wrong if he has to use his fingers to precipitate a climax on the wife's part. The possibilities are numerous.

The third category is even more complicated. Suppose the husband wishes mouth-genital relationship or even penis-rectum experience. He may enjoy the relationship more if the wife is on top in the sexual act. Some people regard these practices as abnormal.

What are we to think of such matters? The question of "abnormal" is one that the counselor and the counselee need to face objectively. If the pastor approaches these problems from a very nonjudgmental viewpoint, some sensible solution may be found.

The really complex problems, relating to the deeper levels of the personality, are the ones which involve triangles. A man or woman becomes involved with a third party. Sexual relations may or may not be involved. All sorts of allegations about platonic love or companionship may enter the picture. The important questions center around such questions as: Why did this occur? What effect does it have on the mate? Is the involved mate willing to terminate the relationship? Can the innocent mate forgive or will she (or he) retaliate later? What is wrong that should be righted in the marriage situation? Are the wounds so deep that they will never heal? Is the attachment one that, though broken, cannot be gotten over? Can the wounded mate expect this to recur or has the offending one learned his lesson?

Finding the answers to these questions and a working approach to changed behavior takes time and patience. Many people cannot be frank at first about how they feel about sexual matters. A wife may talk about the fact that her husband demands sex too often; two or three interviews later she may open up and say that he insists on mouth-genital sex play and that this is terribly offensive to her. Or a husband may say that he does not know why he comes home "loaded" with alcohol; later he may admit that this is the only way he can stand the rebuff of being turned down sexually. Either the man or the woman may be deterred in their sexual response because of fear of pregnancy.

The minister can be of best help to couples if he can define for himself his own philosophy of sex, and if he can interpret the deeper meaning of what sex should mean.

Dietrich Bonhoeffer points out that according to the Biblical conception of marriage, the purpose of sex is not reproduction but the union of man and woman (Gen. 2:18, 23): "For biblical thought this [the command to fruitfulness] would have been impossible; it was only in the age of rationalism and technology that it could come to be understood in this way."[3] In both the Old and New Testaments, sexual enjoyment is looked upon as a natural and wholesome

[3] *Ethics* (New York: The Macmillan Company, 1955), p. 134.

part of marriage (*cf.* 1 Cor. 7.3 ff). The sin of Onan in Genesis 38 has nothing to do with masturbation or birth control but was the unlawful refusal of a brother to provide his dead brother with the offspring which, according to their laws, he owed to him.[4]

From a practical standpoint, the minister should approach sexual problems with the kind of openness to variations that the following propositions afford:

1. Sexual play and sexual relations within the marriage are for enjoyment, mutual pleasure, and self-fulfillment.
2. Any kind of sexual expression between the two is good and right, to be enjoyed without guilt feelings, if it is mutually satisfying.
3. Sexual interchange is to be considered as an act of self-giving and communication between the couple and should not be approached from the standpoint of duty or "giving in."
4. If failures to achieve reasonable mutual satisfactions in sex are present, they must be understood in the light of each person's background and psychological makeup, not simply from an ethical or moralistic viewpoint.
5. In cases of extramarital affairs, ethics are involved, of course, but primary consideration belongs to the causes and cures that encompass the total relationship between the two, as well as the treatment (or counseling) of the one who violates the marriage vows.

The types of variations in the sexual behavior of human beings are many. The important point for ministers is that, once offenses or misunderstandings have occurred, the problems must be faced in terms of more satisfactory relations in the future. It is not a matter of being either broad-minded or legalistic. How can these two people find a better way of meeting each other's needs? This is the important question.

WHERE FORGIVENESS IS NEEDED

A typical example of the need for forgiveness is seen in cases of unfaithfulness. This does not apply to all unfaithfulness. If the rov-

[4] For further discussion of the Christian view of sex, see: Derrick Sherwin Bailey, *Sexual Relation in Christian Thought* (New York: Harper & Row, Publishers, 1959); William Graham Cole, *Sex and Love in the Bible* (New York: Association Press, 1959); and W. Melville Capper and H. Morgan Williams, *Toward Christian Marriage* (Chicago: Inter-Varsity Press, 1958).

ing one does not wish to return to the fold, or wishes both to have his cake and eat it (*i.e.*, to keep both his mate and the lover), or has no intention of changing his behavior or has no concern for the hurt that unfaithfulness has caused, to talk of forgiveness is absurd. In such cases, it is a matter of terminating the marital relation or of accepting the behavior and not making an issue of it.

Forgiveness is possible only in cases where the one who has sinned sees the error of his ways and wishes to rebuild the marital relationship on a sound, predictable pattern of behavior. It means that the erring one must become responsible. The word *responsible*, it should be remembered, comes from *spondere*, "to promise," and *re*, meaning "again." One who becomes responsible assumes the obligation to choose, to decide, to act according to an agreed behavior. If one is so immature that he cannot assume responsibility for himself, or so sick that he says, "I don't know what I might do," forgiveness is not a possibility.

Forgiveness allows a relationship which has been broken to be rebuilt. Two people who have been pulled apart by an event in which one has hurt the other decide to re-relate in a manner that does not involve the estranging event.

What is done with the estranging event? Can it be forgotten or undone? Not at all. When a person says, "I can forgive but I won't forget," the response is, "Of course not! That is not the point. Can you act toward him in a loving manner that more or less ignores what has happened?"

There is a widespread belief in our culture that if a person punishes himself by "feeling bad" about his sins, he is less likely to repeat them. This is probably the opposite to the truth. Self-punishment often paves the way for repetition of the bad act. It may serve as a kind of atonement or expiation, in the guilty one's mind. What really matters is the rebuilding of a new relationship which will be too strong to be broken by infidelity.

So far as the offender is concerned, the counselor must not consider him safe until he has understood something of why he fell into sin and until he has made some realistic decisions about building a deeper relationship with his mate.

Albert Ellis has made a strong case for the fact that self-blame and a feeling of worthlessness may do more harm than good in bring-

ing about reform. He says that such feelings bring about one or more
of four very unfortunate results:

> (1) a deep-seated feeling of personal worthlessness; (2) an obses-
> sive-compulsive occupation with and possible performance of the
> wrong act for which he is blaming himself; (3) denial or repression
> of the fact that his immoral act was actually committed by him, and
> (4) psychopathic insistence that the act was committed but was not
> really wrong.[5]

What he does not appear to see, it seems to me, is that a person may
repent of sin and seek forgiveness without losing respect for himself
as a finite person. I agree with him, however, that the counselor's
primary task is to help the counselee to answer the question: "How
do I *not* repeat this wrong deed next time?"[6]

NOT-IN-LOVE PROBLEMS

A Navy chaplain wrote:

> I'm constantly faced with the Navy wives who are struggling
> with the problem of not feeling right toward their husbands. They
> say, "I just don't love him anymore; what does a person do when
> he has fallen out of love?" This has me puzzled. I know people
> change, but what can you say to a person who says, "I don't love
> my wife anymore"?

This is a problem every marriage counselor faces. Sometimes it is
serious and is indicative of some deep emotional disturbance in the
individual which keeps him from loving anyone with naturalness and
freedom. Again, it may be an alibi for getting out of a marriage
which is fundamentally unrewarding. It may even be a kind of depressive reaction in which a very guilt-ridden person feels the need to
be hurt or doesn't feel worthy to be loved by anyone and is merely
using, "I don't feel anything for him" as a way of getting punished.

The pastor, like any other marriage counselor, must have some
kind of concept of what married love is expected to be. In other
words, what is a man supposed to mean when he says, "I feel that
I love my wife." Certainly, it is some kind of positive feeling. He

[5] "There Is No Place for the Concept of Sin in Psychotherapy," *Journal of
Counseling Psychology,* Vol. 7, No. 3 (1960).
[6] *Idem.*

may even say, "I love her but I don't like her." If he is extremely immature, he may think of love as the kind of romantic crush he had on her in his teenage period.

Love always involves seeing the other person as unique, accepting this fact, opening to and communicating with the other, showing concern for the other's self-fulfillment, and appreciating the other person. Perhaps these terms are too cold. Love is always warm—it is an out-going action, acting in a loving manner.

In our culture, however, a young person often says, "I love you," but means, "I love me and I want you." This leads some writers to taboo romantic love as "bogus romance," "Hollywood love" or "obsessional neurosis." It is this type of love that James Thurber describes as "the strange bewilderment which overtakes one person on account of another person."[7]

With these varieties of love-understandings in mind, what is the pastor to say to one of a couple, or sometimes both, who report "I don't love him (her) anymore"? Perhaps no two marriages have the same love components. And any marriage goes through various stages of love. Love waxes and wanes.

The marriage counselor will explore: (1) how they used to feel and act toward each other; (2) what each understood as the expected love-response as they moved along in the marriage; (3) what happened as the love waned or seemed to, on the part of one or both; (4) what may have been the causal factors in the death of love; (5) whether or not the two wish to or hope to rebuild their love life, and (6) how they can take steps to rebuild a loving relationship.

Unless there is a significant personality impairment, such as extreme insensitivity or pronounced suspicion, two people can usually rebuild a love life, if they once had one, provided both will work at the matter sensibly. One finds, though, in marriage counseling, that love means about as many different things as there are different people. The counselor can only serve as catalyst to release the love two people are capable of giving. But the problem is giving; love is learning to act sincerely and consciously in a loving manner.

What the marriage counselor does, in helping a couple to find mature love, may determine the destiny of a marriage.

[7] James Thurber and E. B. White, *Is Sex Necessary?* (New York: Harper & Row, Publishers, 1929), p. 36.

SIX

WORKING THROUGH The
DIFFICULT CASES

When it is evident that a couple needs more than first-aid, and that they do not wish to be referred to some other professional source, the pastor must proceed to work through to solution the problems that are presented. This is a painstaking, sometimes long-term job. There is no one way to go about it.

Fiedler has produced some interesting comparative studies which show that the quality of the interpersonal relation between the client and the interviewer are the same for all competent therapists, regardless of their theories. He found that skillful therapists participate fully in the patient's communication and convey a sense of sharing in the patient's feelings.[1] As Donald Glad has said concerning Fiedler's analysis of what takes place in therapy (or counseling):

> This description sounds quite like a warm, accepting friendship where one feels well-loved and understood. It should provide a common baseline for effective learning through which the patient may modify himself in ways that the therapist values. So, one might wonder whether Fiedler has provided definition of the therapy relation as a favorable opportunity for learning.[2]

This is precisely the viewpoint of marriage counseling. The counselee senses that he is accepted by the counselor, regardless of whether his feelings are fear, anger, despair, insecurity or helplessness. This is the alpha and omega of working through the problem.

In the process of counseling, various types of help will be given. There will be *guidance*, used sparingly, in which the pastor

[1] F. E. Fiedler, "Factor Analyses of Psychoanalytic, Non-directive, and Adlerian Therapeutic Relationships," *Journal of Consulting Psychology*, Vol. 15 (1951), pp. 32–38.

[2] Donald D. Glad, *Operational Values in Psychotherapy* (New York: Oxford University Press, 1959), p. 5.

will give suggestions about how the counselee may approach his problem. *Environmental manipulation* may be needed to structure the situation so that stress may be lessened or possible productive patterns may be initiated—an example is to withhold divorce proceedings for further explorations of the situation or to move out of the in-laws' home. The counselee may need *reassurance* concerning the mate's intentions or that a particular sexual practice is not perverse or sinful. Even *persuasion* is in order if a particular counselee is about to make a decision which seems unwise or unrealistic. However, the main part of marriage counseling consists of what Wolberg calls *emotional catharsis and desensitization*.[3] This may, at any point, move into *insight counseling*, in which the individual is confronted by the deeper meanings of his feelings and behavior which he may have hitherto overlooked. This is also called *re-educative* or *reconstructive counseling*. The lines of demarcation are not clear. And in an actual interview the movement from one to the other may be largely uncontrolled and unpredictable.

Donald Glad defines psychotherapy as "any psychological method which is intended to improve the personal or social adjustment of individuals who are aware that the therapist is offering psychological help.[4] This goes for any kind of counseling (or psychotherapy), including pastoral counseling.

If I may borrow from Carl Rogers' "process conception"[5] of psychotherapy and apply it to marriage counseling, we may expect the interview content to move through the following stages:

1. Communication about externals—feelings and personal meanings are neither recognized nor admitted.
2. Exhibition of feelings related to the past.
3. Some awareness of the meanings of inner feelings as possibly contradictory.
4. Exhibition of more intense feelings related to the present and of some responsibility for his own part in his problems.
5. Ownership of inner feelings and expression of desire to be a real self.

[3] Lewis R. Wolberg, *The Technique of Psychotherapy* (New York: Grune and Stratton, 1954), p. 28.

[4] Donald D. Glad, *Operational Values in Psychotherapy* (New York: Oxford University Press, 1959), p. 22.

[5] Carl R. Rogers, *On Becoming a Person* (Boston: Houghton Mifflin Company, 1961), pp. 126–59.

6. Growth of a basic trust in his own experiencing of feelings and an awareness of freedom from past ways of feeling and acting.
7. The choosing of new ways of being.

The above movements are illustrated in the case of Jack and Alice James, ages 36 and 34, respectively, married ten years, and the parents of two children.

Alice had become involved emotionally and sexually with the bread man. This, the husband alleged, was not the only problem they had. They had had continued arguments about money and even the night before they came to the counselor, when she had admitted the romantic episode with the bread man, she had demanded three-fourths of his salary in return for a divorce. He admitted drinking excessively in his days off from the railway mail service and that she had some grounds for divorce on this account.

The first interview with Alice revealed a rather competitive marriage relationship, more drinking on Jack's part when she quit work six years ago, and a feeling that she was in love with the bread man and wanted to marry him. She claimed that her flirting with the bread man began when a girl friend who ran around with a man other than her husband kept talking about how exciting it was, and that had triggered off a lot of wild feelings. She was not particularly ashamed of the affair even though she had previously gone to church regularly.

Her second interview focused mainly on her childhood and her mother. The product of a broken home, she and her brother were pressured by her mother to make top grades and to save money. When she was about six years of age, her mother had caught her in her brother's clothes and had taken her to a psychologist to see what was the matter with her. She said she was a demon in grade school, often wished she were a boy, would not wear sweaters in high school, hated to go to Sunday School because she had to wear dresses and wouldn't go to the high school prom because she would have to wear a formal gown. After high school, she left home to room with some girls, working in the daytime and going to the university at night. Soon she fell in love with a married man who left her to return to his wife and child.

In subsequent interviews she was able to say that she had always felt that no one loved her, except Jack, and that he had a deep attachment to his mother. His mother criticized her for spending money, although it had always been spent on the house and children, never on personal pleasure. She blamed her over-identification with money on her mother who had constantly insisted that she save money.

At the end of sixteen interviews, the two got a fairly peaceful divorce. In the meantime Jack had discussed his skin rash which erupted every time he got around his mother, an impotency problem which started two years before, his drinking, and many problems related to his not being able to stand on his own two feet. Alice had gotten a job; broken with her wayward girl friend and the bread man, and had returned to regular church attendance, which she had discontinued during their conflict.

The seventeenth interview (most of these had been with Alice —Jack had been seen occasionally in supportive interviews), Alice related:

> This week I have had some good experiences with people at the office. They all seem closer and it felt good. Also, I am much closer to my little daughter. She must have felt like I used to feel, that nobody really loved her. . . . I have just been playing all of my relationships by ear and not bothering about whether people loved me or not. For the first time in my life I know the difference between feeling and thinking. I can feel now. . . . It has not all been easy. At times I suffer from loneliness, but I can't bemoan the fact, because I know now that I brought it on myself in the way I treated Jack. . . . I know now that I want to become a good person and give to people instead of controlling them or competing with them. Where did I get this feeling that I must always win arguments?

The twentieth interview brought forth the following statements:

> A former neighbor called me up and wanted to date me. I told him that I didn't think it was a good idea, that Jack and I were still going together even though we were divorced. It wasn't the least bit of trouble to tell him. . . . Looking back I don't know why I ever had such a desire to run around. Yes, I do know, too. I was bored. I think my job has been good for me. It makes me feel like I am doing something worthwhile. . . . Jack's mother called up the other night, just to see how I was. You know I don't dislike her anymore. In a way I feel sorry for her. She has no one but Jack. I told her I hoped she wouldn't get Jack all riled up because he might

go out and drink. The next night Jack came by. He and his mother had a big fight and he really told her off. You should have seen him, all smiles; you would have thought that he had just fallen heir to some money. He said he told her off and he didn't feel the least bit guilty about it. . . . Jack and I are having sex now. I don't know what you will think about it. Come to think of it you told me to think for myself. Why should I be concerned for what you think? And you know he does not have any impotency problem. I think I must have been most of the cause of his problem. Even in other things besides sex I was always competing. If we bowled together I would always bowl away above my average score.

After twenty-four interviews, Jack and Alice had restructured their relationship with their mothers, found an approach to money problems, to their children, to friends and to church. Jack's drinking was no longer a problem. Alice was enjoying her work, and he was helping her with the housework. They were remarried in a quiet home wedding. Both had come to feel themselves as persons, to manage their emotions and to make constructive decisions.

The first sixteen interviews were spent largely in the first three stages of the counseling process, as outlined above. But even in this period there were what Rogers called "moments of movement."

At one point in the seventeenth session, I said, "What would you do if Jack were to marry tomorrow? I mean, about your counseling?"

"For the kids' sake I think I would continue. I know I have not worked my problems through."

"But not for yourself?" I asked.

She hesitated. "I guess," she replied, "I have not really thought enough of myself in the past. Everybody has told me how selfish I was, but I don't think it has been the right kind of selfishness."

My answer: "Is it selfish to want to be your complete self?"

Getting a divorce and remarrying may not seem the best solution to many people. It certainly was not my idea, but it was the way these two found their solutions. It is doubtful whether Jack could have ever forgiven Alice if he had not retaliated by divorcing her. Then he was free to see her afresh or to look some other way. If he had not become a man by standing up to both his mother and to Alice, she would probably not have remarried him. If they had remarried without counseling, they would have been right back on the same merry-go-round. Now, after three years, a follow-up indicates that they have continued to build a rich relationship.

LOOKING AT THE DEVELOPMENTAL BACKGROUNDS

In working through such cases, certain aspects of the two individuals must come to light and be dealt with. The most obvious one is the developmental backgrounds of each. Some of this material will come to light in the first or second interview. Often, however, the more significant facts will be withheld until some working approach is found to the crisis which brought the couple to the pastor in the first place. If only the crisis is to be dealt with, without any perception of personality differences, one may be fairly sure that other crises will occur later, and that the marriage will be in jeopardy again.

How are significant background materials to be brought to light? Certainly not by detailed probing into history or feelings. Questions put at the right time as some troubled area is introduced may get the desired result. Such questions may be: "How do you account for such a strong reaction on your part?" "Did you ever have this feeling before?" "Is this the way you would have reacted to your father?" "Have you had this feeling of worthlessness most of your life?" "It sounds to me as if he triggered off some resentments that have been there for a long time; do you remember feeling this before you married?"

As people talk about their painful experiences, they tend to feel less strongly about them. Or they become desensitized to them. Or they come to accept feelings for what they are and act more rationally concerning them. They may even find that they can express feelings, even negative feelings, without breaking a relationship.

A twenty-five-year-old woman who responded poorly to her husband in sex relations kept recounting that she felt that sex was all he wanted of her. She hinted at the fact she had felt very much that way in her dating period, that boys were trying to "get" to her. After the counseling relationship was solidly established, I said to her, "You know, you sound to me like a woman who has been attacked or approached sexually when you were a child. Do you remember anything like this happening to you?"

A brief silence transpired, followed by a burst of tears and sobs. Then she told me that when she was about twelve her stepfather had come into her room and played with her sexually. She was able to see that this experience had colored her view of men through the years, that she had tended to see all of them as seducers. As she talked about it—she had never told anyone before—it became less painful, and she was able to talk freely about her own sexual and affectional needs and began to relate more wholesomely to her husband. In the meantime, with her permission, I was able to communicate some of her problems concerning sex to her husband. He became more permissive and less pushy, which took him out of the stepfather role.

In order to understand two people in marital conflict, it is imperative that their backgrounds be discussed. The counselor's role is perceiving what aspects are pertinent and what recounting of history is merely a coverup in order to avoid facing current problems. He may need to say, "But I do not see what that has to do with what is happening now." If the counselee can justify his account, fine. If not, he may come to understand that he is merely feeling sorry for himself and using his background as an excuse for failure.

HELPING EACH TO FACE HIS IMMATURITIES

It has already been suggested that the term *immature* is often merely a club with which to hit someone over the head. Nevertheless, counselees will bring up the term, and it does have some utility.

Wife: After talking to my husband, can't you see that he is just a little boy who has never grown up?

Pastor: He has some real problems, but you will have to admit that he holds a pretty good job.

Wife: Yes I know, but Pastor, you know he's a big baby. Look at the way he acts when my brother comes to see me. You would think that my brother is an old boyfriend.

Pastor: This burns you up, doesn't it?

Wife: I have just never seen anyone as jealous as he is. He just wants to possess me body and soul.

Pastor: Tell me, how do you figure this? How did he get that way? You must know a good deal about his childhood.

Wife: Oh yes, he was a spoiled child and always had his own way. His sister, ten years older, and his mother waited on him hand and foot. And now he expects me to do the same.

Pastor: To me the problem seems to be a very critical one. He seems to need more than you can give, and becomes angry when you do not meet his demands. On the other hand the only approach you have found is to judge him, to call him immature. Is there no other approach to this problem?

Wife: Is that what I am doing, judging him?

Pastor: It seems so to me. You seem to have lost respect for him, to think of him as immature, as a little boy. Isn't that judging him, in a way?

Wife: I guess that is judging him. (Pause)

Pastor: I wonder if it wouldn't be a better approach to try to understand why this irks you so.

Wife: I think I know the answer to that. My father was one who never could stand weakness of any sort. But I wouldn't want him to be like my father. He was cold and aloof and never got close to anyone.

Pastor: Maybe that is why you married your husband, because he was concerned and warm and easy to get close to.

Wife: Maybe.

Pastor: But your image of strength was already formed when you married, so the very qualities which drew you to your husband later repelled you and even disgusted you.

Wife: I can't stand his possessiveness.

Pastor: Let me talk to him next time and see if I can understand what he is doing. Maybe he can find a better way. In the meantime, see if you can understand why his traits bother you so much.

Later, in talking with the husband, the same material entered into the interview:

Husband: I never have been able to get close to Irene. She is so independent and selfish. She doesn't seem to care what anyone else feels or thinks.

Pastor: Just how close do you want to be?

Husband: Why, you never know what she is thinking. It's almost like living in the house with a stranger.

Pastor: And this makes you feel that she doesn't love you?

Husband: Yeah, how would you feel if your wife could talk to everyone but you? The minute people walk in the door she is all sparkles and smiles. When they leave, she is as glum as a wooden Indian.

Pastor: I got the impression from her that she sees you as very much in need of a lot of attention. Perhaps too much?

Husband: All I want is a little kindness. She never tells me that she loves me or believes in me. Never any real expression of feeling.

Pastor: And this would tend to make you a little extractive—sort of trying to extract love from her because you are so hungry?

Husband: I guess it would.

Pastor: It doesn't work, does it?

Husband: Something hasn't.

Pastor: Wouldn't this make her see you as a little boy who is coming around to get a pat on the head.

Husband: That is what she is always telling me, that I am so immature, a spoiled child.

Pastor: Maybe you can find some way to feed yourself emotionally. If trying to get her to say "I love you" puts you in a bad light, you may have to stand taller and assure yourself from within.

Husband: I guess I always thought that marriage was supposed to be love and that a man had a right to expect his wife to take an interest in him.

Pastor: In a way, you are right. But I am not so sure that if a wife really loves her husband, that she has to tell him in so many words. Incidentally, her feeling about this is that you seem to want to possess her or smother her and that this keeps her from being herself.

Husband: Maybe so. I just don't understand it.

Pastor: But you do understand that she sees you as critical of her and reaching out for her too often, don't you? Think this over and see if there is some way for you to assure yourself. Then you will be more comfortable and have more to give. Keep looking at this. Blaming each other will not get the job done.

Such a direct approach may become too threatening to some counselees. Others can be told outright that they received more love as a child than the adult world affords and that emotional gluttony just will not work. In any case, the problem has to be faced, whether gently or harshly. Each counselee must be dealt with in the light of what he can take and depending on the strength of the counselor-counselee relationship.

INTERPRETATION VERSUS CRITICISM

One of the most crucial problems in counseling is deciding when to interpret some behavior pattern and when to confront the counselee with the brutal facts of his existence. Whether we use the term *confrontation, interpretation* or *intervention,* we are dealing with what the counselor introduces into the dialogue which may assist the counselee in understanding himself and in making decisions for himself.

Take, for example, the counselee who says: "Now, Pastor, you have heard both sides; you see how hopeless it is. What do you think I should do about getting a divorce?"

Suitable responses might be: "At this point I am a little puzzled about just how bad the situation is. Can you tell me more about how you feel about him?" or "This is a big decision and I think we ought to look at all angles of this before this question is answered."

The one type of response which the pastor will wish to avoid is that of criticism. This does not mean that he will not confront the individual with what he considers to be the right answer. This is a part of his duty as a counselor. But criticism of the counselee as a person is hardly helpful in marital difficulties.

When the pastor says, "You will be the one who has to find the answer," he is not refusing to help, nor criticizing the counselee for asking the question. He is confronting the counselee with the fact that in making some decisions an individual has to stand completely alone. He is merely refusing to make a decision which belongs only to the individual who is asking the question. Instead of interpreting the marital crisis, he is interpreting the human situation—as it applies to this condition or to any other—that each one of us must decide for himself.

As Rollo May has pointed out concerning decisions, whether these are made by the counselor or counselee, they may be a short cut to avoid anxiety, that "to act may be easier and may quiet anxiety more quickly than the slow, arduous process of self exploration."[6] The point is especially applicable to marriage counseling. Premature jumping to a decision, such as divorce or even staying in the marriage, is much less likely to lead to a satisfying life than a painstaking working through of the problems involved. In other words, bearing the anxiety of not knowing where the interviews are coming out is, for both the counselor and the counselees, a necessary part of good conclusions.

Interpreting or confronting may be of real value under the following circumstances:

1. When it focuses on the reality factors involved.
   Example: When a husband says that he will sue for the custody of the children when the chances are a thousand to one that he would not dare go into court with such a suit, but is merely bluffing.

2. When emotional factors are obviously distorting the picture.
   Example: A man who is sure that his wife is unfaithful because of unexplained mileage on the car speedometer, or a woman who blows up because she has found telephone numbers in her husband's billfold.

3. When arguments center around events and it becomes obvious that the real problem is the total interpersonal pattern.
   Example: A husband who sees his wife kiss another man at the Christmas office party but really has not felt loved by her all year.

4. When ignorance is involved and the facts need to be brought into the picture.
   Example: A husband who has had all the children he and his wife wish to bring into the world, but has heard that a vasectomy causes the husband to get fat and pudgy and may even kill desire.

5. When the focus is on the mate's behavior, such as "he un-

[6] *Existence* (New York: Basic Books, Inc., 1958), p. 88.

dermines my self-esteem," when the individual counselee has never had self-esteem.

Example: The woman who says, "My husband never notices anything new that I have on and never compliments me for anything I do." Why does she not learn to compliment herself?

6. When the counselee continues to talk about the past instead of the present and the future.

Example: The wife who rehearses the bloody details of a fight they had while both were drinking and overlooks their years of good times together, and the basic character of her husband.

7. When the focus is entirely on the errors and faults of one, without any awareness of how the other might have contributed.

Example: The husband who insists on stopping at the tavern for a few beers because otherwise he could not stand his wife's bad temper.

8. When one does not wish to save the marriage and the other cannot accept this fact.

Example: A man who is homosexual and has discovered within the marriage how loathsome the feminine body is to him, but does not wish to try to become heterosexual.

These, of course, do not exhaust the possibilities of types of situations where confrontation is essential. It certainly does not say how it can be done without creating too much anxiety, giving the impression of rejecting, blaming, ridiculing or belittling the counselee, thus destroying the counseling relationship.

Confronting is an art. It can only be learned by experience, preferably under supervision. No rules are possible. Good sense, honesty, sincerity and empathy are the necessary prerequisites.

MAINTAINING POSITIVE RELATIONSHIP IN COUNSELING

Some marriage counselors stress the relationship between the counselor and the counselees. Psychoanalysis, for example, makes this a primary focus. Whether we speak of *transference*—the reenactment of an earlier relationship with a parent or parents; or whether we think in terms of roles—policeman, teacher, doctor, scholar, brother, uncle, lover, friend or nurse, we cannot avoid being in various relationships with the counselee. This relationship must be under constant surveillance by the counselor.

Unless the minister can be sure that he will not become romantically involved and fall into the role of a lover or marriage partner, he should either refrain from marriage counseling altogether or seek counsel himself to work through his own emotional problems.

What, then, is the positive relationship that the pastor must maintain throughout the vissicitudes of the counseling process? Actually, his role should be more that of a father or brother or friend.

Maslow describes the "good human relationship" of psychotherapy as identical with any other good relationship—husband-wife, parent-child or friendship—as "the giving of safety, love, belongingness, feeling of worth and self-esteem."[7] The counselees are members of the "community of God," or potentially so, and are therefore valuable and to be respected and left free under God. In some churches, the pastor will be more in the "father" role and may even be addressed as "Father." In the more democratic or so-called "free churches," his role may be more that of a "brother."

In marriage counseling, or any other counseling, the minister must point the counselee's feelings to him again and again, interpret what he is saying or doing in the counseling relationship and in others, emphasize the importance of his making clean-cut decisions for himself, and indicate what it means to respect oneself as a decider. In this way the counselee gains a feeling of worth and self-esteem which no amount of outside help can instill. The relationship remains positive because two people are looking at the alternate choices and their consequences together, without one having all the answers and the other taking all of the consequences.

WHEN AND HOW TO TERMINATE

The most common fault of ministers as marriage counselors is that they resort to "quickie solutions" and terminate the series of

[7] A. H. Maslow, *Motivation and Personality* (New York: Harper & Row, Publishers, 1954), p. 313.

interviews before anything significant has happened. This is partly due, no doubt, to the pressure of the schedule under which the minister operates. We tend to leave couples half-cured, like the blind man whom Jesus restored (Mark: 8). At one point the man said, "I see men; but they look like trees, walking." Jesus laid his hands upon his eyes. Then, the Scripture says, he "was restored and saw everything clearly."

The implication here is not that every counselee should work out all of his neurotic problems before his case is terminated, but, rather, that he should see clearly where the problems in his interpersonal relations lie, and at least get the "feel" of better relationships and have some idea of where to go from there. Many counselees will themselves terminate before they have gotten that far because of anxiety, childish optimism, indifference, etc.

Nevertheless, the counselor must decide how much help each couple or individual needs and how this is to be interpreted to them or to him. If they have seen some of their major problems and each has found a working approach to the other, how is the counselor to approach the matter of termination?

The easiest termination process is one in which the counselee brings it up himself.

A second type of termination is one that involves resistance on the part of the counselees to taking help. After all, to take help in looking at ourselves is a sign of weakness to many people in our culture. Besides being painful and face-losing at points, there is a popular idea that only the weak seek help. When the attempt to terminate is seen by the counselor as resistance to change, he should try to help them see it:

> *Wife:* I can't see that talking about this is doing any good. If you do not mind, I think today will be the last visit.
>
> *Pastor:* I see.
>
> *Wife:* Do you think it is doing any good to talk about our problem?
>
> *Pastor:* This has me a little puzzled at this point. I'm not sure what you are saying.
>
> *Wife:* I just don't see what good it is doing for us to come in here and talk about our problems.

Pastor: Maybe it would help if you say what "good" you are looking for. Are you, perhaps, angry because I don't have a quick solution to your problem or because I won't tell you two what to do?

Wife: Well, we came to you because we felt you would be fair in your decisions. Both of us feel that you have not given us much help. What is counseling for if it is not to arrive at decisions?

Pastor: But whose decisions? Yours or mine? You told me that both your parents and your husband had made decisions for you. And now, if I hear you correctly, you are asking me to do the same. I don't resent this, but I feel that as you talk about your problem you will come to feel that you know what you want to do about your marriage. This is a tremendous decision. I don't blame you for shrinking from making it. But sooner or later you are going to have to make it. If you are not ready, O.K., but let's try to look at what you are feeling at this moment. What is it that you feel? (Pause)

Wife: I guess you are right. Perhaps John and I both were expecting the impossible. (Pause) What am I feeling? I feel that I want you to decide for me and I know at the same time that you ought not do that.

Pastor: Right. And you need to face the fact that you and John have a real problem that must be looked at over and over until you see what is wrong and whether you two really want to make a go of this marriage or whether you want to give up the ship. Are you ready now to get down to the problem?

Wife: (Long pause) I guess we were expecting you to wave a magic wand and solve our problems. It doesn't work that way, does it?

Pastor: No, it doesn't. Why don't you go home and talk to John about what to expect of counseling? Maybe he can see, too, that you two are going to have to use patience in working this through. If he sees it, come back. If not, it will do no good for either of you to come back. You understand that I will be very happy if I can be of help. Talk to him and see what he thinks.

Wife: I know you are right. I want to come back whether he does or not. Do you mind?

Pastor: No, I will be glad to see you. Or him. Talk to him and give me a ring about what he says.

A third type of termination involves the suggestion on the part of the counselor that the time has come for the counseling to end:

Pastor: It occurs to me that you two have come to the point where your counseling should come to an end. How do you feel about it?

Husband: I think we can make it by ourselves now.

Wife: It is all right with me, except I hope he won't start that drinking again. I can't stand that.

Pastor: Do you see a little more clearly why he drank?

Wife: I think so. It was partly my fault. I know that I nagged a lot and was hard to live with.

Pastor: (To husband) And do you see that drinking did not solve the problem and that there may be a better way to handle the problem?

Husband: Yes, I can handle the drinking. I have told her that she doesn't need to worry about that.

Pastor: But what are you going to do about the resentment? There still has to be some other way to handle it. She will not be perfect, you know.

Husband: Yes, I know. But if we can do things together and can talk about our problems I don't think I will feel resentful. (Turns to wife) She hasn't been as bad as I made her out. I guess I just got a lot of things inside me that I couldn't get out. I see now that it wasn't all her fault.

Pastor: Why don't you two work on this for a month and see if you can keep the channels of communication open. At the end of a month let's sit down and talk about how you are doing. A kind of checkup to see whether or not you are still moving in the right direction.

However the counseling sessions are ended, the feeling on the part of both counselor and counselee should be that of optimism. Generally, there should be mutual agreement as to the appropriateness and the manner of termination.

SEVEN

The MORE HOPEFUL CASES

The word *hopeful* needs to be defined. One way would be to ascertain: hopeful of what? Naturally, the pastor, with his idea of the sacredness and permanency of marriage, will tend to be hopeful that the marriage can be maintained and made a good one—good for both partners and for the children, if there are any. But what is the hope in case the marriage is depriving, destructive, even devastating, to the two people involved? And what if the children are being deformed (psychologically or spiritually) by the marital difficulties? In these cases, the hope is that the two will decide to get as clean a divorce as possible and will do so without too many guilt feelings.

Hopeful, therefore, must be defined in terms of self-fulfillment. Can these two people fulfill themselves, find reasonable satisfactions in life, in the marriage relationship? Or, are they doomed to live in a very limited (who is to say how limited?) marriage? Can they live in the marriage without tragic outcomes such as extreme poverty; adulterous relationships with its attendant disgraces and humiliations; bodily or emotional injury, or even spiritual destruction? This does not mean that a marriage has to be happy or successful in every area. Few ministers, however, would feel that a marriage should be maintained if it is unfulfilling in several important aspects—companionship, sex, economic security, children, identity, etc.

Which cases, then, can the pastoral counselor or any other marriage counselor expect to help? This will depend on two big factors: the equipment, training, skills and personality of the counselor; and the maturity, flexibility, openness, even intelligence and motivation of the counselees. We shall attempt, in the following discussion, to suggest some of the more hopeful types of cases which turn to a pastor for help.

RESTRUCTURING RELATIONSHIPS
WITH IN-LAWS

In our Western culture, influenced by the Judeo-Christian tradition, we have a framework for familial relationships which spells out how a new couple shall start a new home: "A man shall leave his father and mother and be joined to his wife" (Matt. 19:5 and elsewhere). It is assumed that the same applies to the wife.

But this does not answer such important questions as: Shall he leave them emotionally? How far away (geographically) shall they live? How often shall he (or she) return for visits? Should each go alone to see his (or her) parents? How often should the parents visit their children and how long should they stay? Who is to decide these matters?

There are many studies to show that problems with in-laws can be acute, though perhaps not as acute as popular jokes and magazine articles would indicate. The pastor will find them lurking in the background of many other conflictual situations as a contributing factor. He will find in-laws as the focal point of disagreement in many cases.

Typical in-law problems revolve around such matters as accepting financial help from one or both of the parents, deciding which parents to visit on holidays, living close to or in the house with one set of parents, and the like. The principles, however, are the same as counseling in other types of problems: understanding what each feels in the light of his background, clarifying feelings that have lain dormant, experimenting with new approaches to the in-laws and helping each of the two to move toward autonomy and cooperation.

WHEN LOVE HAS WANED

In Chapter Five, we suggested some aspects of the "Not-in-love Problems" that should be explored by the counselor, and the variety of meanings that love has in our culture. Here I would like to demonstrate how one counselee moved from the feeling that she did not love her husband to one of warmth and acceptance which became enriching to both. Only a few excerpts from the counseling dialogue are included:

Wife: Like I told you last time, I just don't love Jimmy and I don't know what to do about it. I hate to say the same thing over and over. If it wasn't for hurting him I would leave him. He says he will give me a divorce, but I know that he loves me, and I don't know what to do about it.

Pastor: How do you mean "hurting him"? He is a grown man. Why do you have to feel sorry for him? Does he act that helpless?

Wife: Well, he says he will do anything to win me back. I really don't dislike him as a person, but I just don't feel anything for him. As I told you last time, I thought I loved him when I married him, but I just don't feel that way anymore.

Pastor: And you think you are doing him a favor by staying with him?

Wife: Well, that is what I have been trying to decide. This is a heck of a position to be in. Spending three years with a man and then tell him that you don't love him.

Pastor: It makes you feel like a dirty dog?

Wife: Worse than that. I just don't want to hurt him.

Pastor: Why don't you let me talk to him and see what he thinks. In the meantime, I would like for you to think about what you are looking for. Here is a man who is devoted to you and adores you, and you say that you don't dislike him as a person and that you are not in love with anyone else. It sounds to me as if you do not know how to love anyone. I'm not being critical of you for this, but if this is the problem we need to face it.

An interview with the husband revealed that he was not nearly as helpless as she had pictured him. He was very mature about the whole thing. We agreed that his approach should be one of backing away from her and telling her very matter-of-factly that if she wanted a divorce or a separation period, he would be glad to give it to her. He felt that if the marriage had been a mistake, now was the time to face it. In this stronger position, in her eyes, he was better able to create a framework within which she could make a decision.

When she came in the next time, the following dialogue took place:

Wife: I don't know what you did to my husband, but he sure has changed.

Pastor: Oh?

Wife: I guess I was wrong about him. He not only seems stronger, but he even showed some anger. It's the first time I have seen him really show spunk. He told me that if I didn't love him, it was about time that he find it out and get out and find someone who did love him.

Pastor: How did that make you feel?

Wife: I don't know. I guess I was puzzled. Now, I don't know what to think. (Pause) You said something last time about my not loving anyone. I've been thinking about that. I guess I never have loved anyone very deeply. Do you suppose that is what is the matter with me?

Pastor: What do you think?

Wife: Well, it's a pretty horrible thought. It makes you feel that you are some kind of an oddball or something. (Long pause) Is this something you can learn, I mean to love someone?

Pastor: You are wondering if I think you are some kind of an oddball?

Wife: I was just wondering if there is hope for a person like me. Can people learn to love after they are grown, or is this something you learn in childhood?

Pastor: Is there any hope, huh?

Wife: Yeah, maybe some people just love more than others, and maybe I am the kind who just does not have any deep feelings.

Pastor: Do you really believe this?

Wife: Well, now isn't it true that some people can love better than others, just have more warmth?

Pastor: Why do you keep generalizing about the way people are? Isn't the real question how you are? Do you think that you are a hopeless, cold potato? Or is this simply some kind of defense you have built up against getting hurt?

Wife: What am I afraid of?

Pastor: Yes, what *are* you afraid of?

Wife: That's funny that you should put it that way, because I have always felt that if I ever loved anyone or anything deeply, that I would lose it. (Cries) I don't know why I should feel that way. The only thing I ever remember losing was my little dog when I was about five years old; I guess I was. He got run over. It is silly to feel that way.

Pastor: Silly to feel sorrow over losing your little dog? What kind of talk is that? When you are five years old and love your little dog, losing him can be a major tragedy. I don't understand what you are saying.

Wife: I guess I have always been ashamed of my emotions.

Pastor: Yes, even the emotions connected with love. So you just squelch these emotions and then sit there and say, "I don't love my husband and I don't know why I don't." How could you love when you have made up your mind never to love anybody or anything again like you loved that little dog? You don't dare to love!

Wife: Is that why I don't love my husband?

Pastor: You don't dare love. You might get hurt. Doesn't that make sense: I noticed when you cried that you seemed ashamed of your tears. Are tears anything to be ashamed of?

Wife: I guess I got that from my mother. . . .

From there the conversation moved back to recounting more history and more about her mother who had a pose or front of strength and could not stand weakness. Then she switched back to talking about her husband and how he always saw her as a pillar of strength. She admitted that she was not strong and wanted to be weak at times like other people. When she left she breathed a sigh of relief and said, "Somehow I feel better. Maybe I have been putting up a front like my mother."

In subsequent interviews she was able to talk of some of the weaknesses she saw in her husband, of her own weaknesses, of how she could turn loose some of her emotions, both positive and negative, and of what kind of a feeling human being she wanted to be. The question of whether or not she loved her husband fell into the background, and she began to deal more and more with how she related to people, and even to God. She was even able to tell me that she felt close to me and was not ashamed to put it into words.

She recounted a dream in which she had written me a love poem, could remember all eight lines of it, and it was addressed to me. In the dream she was reading it to me. She accepted the fact that these were feelings which she never was able to express to her father, and that it was good to feel for someone and know that it was accepted in the right manner.

At the end of twenty interviews (four of which were with the husband), she felt that she had a working relationship with her husband, that he was a fine man, and that she could act in a loving manner, sincerely, without debating the question of whether or not she loved him in some particular manner.

There are many other types of "love" problems which the marriage counselor must face. Sometimes the person who says, "I don't love my mate," has already fallen in love with someone else but is unwilling to admit it. Others have built up so much resentment to the mate that positive feelings have been repressed. Still others have simply let love die by failure to express it. Each must be dealt with in the light of the dynamics involved.

THOSE WITH SEXUAL DIFFICULTIES

Except in cases of frank perversions, sexual problems are often solvable, and the pastor, since he is an authority figure in moral matters, is in a good position to help. It should be admitted, however, that in repeated and long-term unfaithfulness and promiscuity, we are often dealing with a repressed homosexual or a person who is sociopathic (has a character disorder); and such cases will be dealt with in the chapter on "Which Cases Are Hopeless?"

Many people talk about sexual problems when their real problems are such matters as anger, resentment, vanity (narcissism), insecurity or jealousy. Others focus on such problems as money, in-laws, discipline of the children or recreation, when all of these could be handled if they were responding sexually to each other in a satisfactory manner. The evaluation of what the major problem is, and what minor problems cause it or cluster about it or obscure it, is not a simple one. The wisest procedure for the marriage counselor is to start with the presenting problem and take it at face value until the deeper problems turn up in the course of counseling.

Take *frigidity* problems. These will be worded in such terms as: "My wife is not affectionate," "She lies passive all through the sexual act," "She does not reach a climax or orgasm," "She does not seem to enjoy having sex" or "She finds pain or displeasure in intercourse." A wide variety of problems are included under this heading.

Mrs. A, 39, came to the pastor saying that her husband often complained of her coldness. So far as she knew she had never experienced a climax, and she wondered what was wrong with her. Reared in a very rigid and conservative religious family where sex was never mentioned, she entered marriage completely ignorant of sexual matters. As she talked of her upbringing she was aware that pleasure of a genital nature was understood by her as taboo. She had never conceived of sex as something to be enjoyed by the woman, but something to be endured. Later, when she had achieved orgastic pleasure she said that the concepts which had freed her were those of "throwing yourself into the sexual experience" and of "abandonment." Likely the freeing factors were that in discussing sexual matters she had gotten the permission of her conscience to enjoy sex. The pastor had said to her, "Why don't you think of doing the thing, expressing yourself in the manner, that will bring you the greatest pleasure?" This to her, formerly, would have been selfish. She learned, of course, that when she "let go" she brought extreme delight to her husband.

An interview with the husband revealed that he had almost no concept of the importance of love play. As he took time to stimulate her and prove to her that he wished to bring her pleasure, she found it easier to respond spontaneously.

Soon the wife reported that she had been "unlocked" and that they were experiencing a new honeymoon, one much more satisfying than their first one, and that she needed no further help because both of them were satisfied with their new-found communication or communion.

Often a wife's apparent coldness or reticence concerning sex can be found to center around her fear of pregnancy or of being hurt in the sexual act, her preconceptions that women are not to appear passionate, her hostility toward the male generally or specific disturbances in interpersonal relations between her and her husband.

Whatever the causes of frigidity on the part of the woman (except physiological ones) usually the situation will not be changed unless the total relationship between the two is explored and the hidden causes uncovered. Usually medicines, shots and the like, do little good. As two people work patiently to free themselves from past blocks formed by culturally determined guilt feelings and by feelings of inadequacy, they can find mutually satisfying ways of communing with each other in intimate relations.

Impotency in the male, however, is a different matter. If it is frequent or long-standing, the prognosis is not so hopeful. The many variations of this type of emotional disturbance make it even more puzzling when it crops up in the counseling interview. Some men ejaculate prematurely, cannot hold back, and thereby deprive their mates. Premature ejaculation is usually caused by a fear of impotency. Some lose the erection before satisfaction for either is reached. Some men can function perfectly with a prostitute, but fail completely with their mates or with a woman whom they respect.

Inasmuch as impotence is so closely related to some of the deepest fears of a man—fear of losing independence, castration anxiety and even fear of death—the complete recovery of the individual is much more complicated. The pastoral counselor will usually wish to refer chronic impotency cases to professional counselors. Where intermittent impotency has occurred in the marriage relationship, and not over a long period, however, the condition may be helped by exploring such areas as the man's image of himself, his guilt feelings about sexual pleasure, his feelings of inadequacy, his fear of failure, his over-concern for pleasing the mate and especially his views of women in general.

The deep commitment and involvement of two persons in marriage, which is the minister's genuine concern if he knows his Bible, cannot overlook the importance of sex. If he can assist them in finding out who they are and how they are to be-in-relatedness within the marital bond, he is fulfilling his function as a minister.

In sex the husband and wife are deeply involved, abandoned, committed and completely open to each other. Whatever retards this relatedness is a challenge to the pastoral counselor in his helping people to self-fulfillment.

COMMUNICATION AS THE MAIN PROBLEM

Logically, this discussion follows that concerning sexual problems because sex is primarily communication, not mere physical gratification; and there are few matters in marriage about which couples have such difficulty in communicating as in sex.

"I didn't know he felt that way," a counselor will often hear a woman say. Or "We cannot ever talk things out; it always ends in an argument."

The most hopeful types of marriage problems involving communication are those where the following characteristics are present:

1. Each will admit that he has contributed to the problem.
2. Each is willing to change if someone can show some feasible way to do so.
3. Each will talk without using emotionally loaded words, such as *childish, selfish* and *silly*.
4. Each will refrain form "psychologizing" about why the other behaves as he does.
5. Each will take responsibility for managing his own emotions—not "he makes me mad" but when he says so-and-so "I let myself get mad."
6. Each will refrain from re-runs on old arguments.
7. Each will focus on one problem at a time and not dash off to peripheral problems.
8. Each will learn to deal with the present and the future instead of the past.
9. Each will express positive feelings toward the other instead of majoring on negative feelings.
10. Each will learn to communicate in nonverbal ways, such as touching, patting, kissing and other forms of skin-to-skin relationship.

Marriage counseling often results in a couple's being able to discuss their thoughts, feelings, and hopes which heretofore had been kept in the background. Talking freely with the counselor, they find out how to express their feelings to each other without attacking each other. The ability to open up to each other is the end result of marriage counseling. Ruth Cavan's statement concerning communication sets a goal for marriage counseling:

> Good communication means simply that husband and wife express their thoughts and relate their activities to each other and that each is ready to listen, understand and respond.[1]

If the feelings, especially positive ones, were included in this definition, it could be said that such communication is both the means to the end and the end of marriage counseling.

[1] *American Marriage* (New York: Thomas Y. Crowell Company, 1959), p. 248.

WHERE ENRICHMENT IS THE REAL NEED

The pastor will often see marriages which are sick or dying without any big, apparent reason. The couples do not fight. They have no focus of conflict, such as sex, in-laws, money or drinking. Neither is in love with anyone else. These marriages simply die, as one pastoral counselor expressed it, of "dry rot."

How can such marriages, and others which are in the process of rebuilding, be enriched? How can these two people find a more meaningful relationship and surround their husband-wife ties with reinforcements which will make them hold under the stress of future crises or stand the wear of day-to-day boredom?

Each pastor will look for enrichment according to his own conceptions of a well-rounded life. The individual must find meaning and significance for himself and in his marriage. Dr. Victor Frankl, the noted psychiatrist, says that this "void, state of inner emptiness, is at present one of the major challenges to psychiatry." He calls it "the existential vacuum":

> Man's struggle for his self and identity is doomed to failure, unless it is enacted as dedication and devotion to something beyond his self, to something above his self. As Jaspers puts it, "What man is, he becomes through that cause which he has made his own."[2]

It seems that this applies equally to individuals and to marriages.

Couples need a cause to live for. This may be found in joining political clubs, in serving on boards of public institutions, in being foster-parents for delinquents, in PTA activities, in lodges and in various community projects. The greatest single outlet for couples seeking to find meaning to their lives is the church. Here are opportunities to work together in teaching, visiting, worshiping and socializing. Even small churches with inadequate programs offer opportunities for service and self-giving which may bring a significance to the family which other agencies do not even claim.

Couples need to play together. Play is something that is done for sheer fun. It has been defined as "something which is nobody's business." Shiller, the German poet, said "Man is perfectly human only when he plays."

[2] Victor E. Frankl, "Psychiatry and Man's Quest for Meaning," *Journal of Religion and Health*, Vol. 1, No. 2 (January 1962), p. 100.

I think I can safely say that between 80 and 90 per cent of the sick marriages which I have dealt with in the last few years are made up of couples who have almost no wholesome, regular play life together. Many of them drink excessively because they do not know how to play. Dr. Karl Menninger says a similar thing about emotionally sick people: "In our work with psychiatric patients we are constantly impressed by the fact that they are deficient in play, or at least that they have never been able to develop balanced recreational techniques."[3]

It can be said without much fear of refutation that "the family that plays together stays together." To revise the original adage is not to belittle prayer in the least.

Again and again I have asked couples what they do for recreation. Too often their reply is, "Oh, we watch television together." If this is all, you can bet that they fight over which channel to turn to.

Couples need friends.   Some need them more than others. I have often seen marriages begin to grow when the estranged or bewildered couple took the initiative to invite another couple over for cards or a meal. Two or three close couples, of the buddy-buddy type relationship, serve as a kind of support to keep a conflictual marriage from flying apart, much as the kinship ties and neighbor relationships did a hundred years ago.

One of the first adjustments of a newly married couple is to find, now that they have moved out of the single group, other young married couples of their own age and preferably of their own interests. Lateral relationships with other couples, close and sincere and deep, tend to keep a couple from becoming bored with each other and to give them some orientation in how other married couples solve their marital problems.

The marriage counselor does not outline the needs for enrichment as a minister outlines his sermon. He brings up the possibility angle, say in finding mutual hobbies and interests, and asks them what they think or feel about this need. Sometimes he may confront them with the irrationality of their deprivations: "No wonder your marriage has failed; you haven't done anything to enrich it. It died of neglect."

If enrichment techniques, experiments with new ways of life,

3 *Love Against Hate* (New York: Harcourt, Brace and World, Inc., 1942), p. 185.

do not seem to work, the pastor must look for deeper emotional causes, either within the individual personalities or within the interaction patterns which the two are practicing.

Our attempt in this chapter has been to suggest that certain types of marriage problems are fairly easily solved if the pastor will attack the problems with the couple forthrightly and realistically. Between these simpler cases and the more hopeless ones are a wide variety of types of problems which only God and human patience can solve. Which problems are solvable will be discovered as the counseling proceeds.

EIGHT

WHEN, WHERE, And HOW To REFER

One of the most delicate problems the minister faces is how to refer people who come to him to some other person who may help.

Sometimes he may simply not wish to deal with a problem because, with his other duties, he plainly does not have time. If he starts dealing with a marriage problem and then cannot find the time to carry it through, he has failed. Indeed, he may even have caused more harm, because when troubled people are disappointed with the help they get they are less likely to seek help elsewhere.

On the other hand, if the minister, even in a comparatively small church, has a number of families in trouble at the same time, he may find himself neglecting his other responsibilities in his efforts to help them. In consequence, he may neglect his own family and thus create personal problems for himself.

Occasionally, there are chronic cases of discontent that he may simply wish to get off his back. Some people expect magic; especially since religion has given people the impression that it has "the" answer to every problem. Wise religious leaders know that some problems have to be lived with. To leave the impression that a "cure" is possible when it is not can do more damage than good. The only honest approach is to confront the counselee with the depth and longstanding aspect of the problem and admit that you see no immediate solution.

WHAT REFERRAL RESOURCES ARE AVAILABLE?

This is the first problem the pastor faces as he moves on a new church field. Such information can be gotten from other pastors, physicians in the community, school officials and lay members of the church.

The first concern will be to find religiously-oriented sources. If these cannot be found, one's next question will be: "Does this person appreciate the value and meaning of religious experience, and can he be depended on not to sabotage the individual's faith or practice?" It is uncomfortable for the pastor to refer a member to someone and have him return later with the report that Dr. So-and-so said that the Bible is simply a book of poetry and is not to be taken seriously.

There are those who claim that a therapist does not have to be religious in order to do good therapy with a religious person. This is true. Counseling, however, cannot help but involve values. If the counselee says, "I have prayed about this matter, and God has told me not to get a divorce," it will be somewhat devastating to the individual if the counselor says, "Personally, I don't believe that God tells people whether or not they should get a divorce." If he says, "You feel very strongly that divorce is not the solution at this point; we will talk about it and see if we can find a solution to your problem," he will come much nearer helping. The question of whether or not the counselor believes in prayer and in guidance is not the primary one. He must at least understand that this is the way some people arrive at their conclusions. After all, who is to say whether or not God does tell people to get or not to get a divorce?

Having ruled out those sources that may have an adverse effect on religion, the pastor must try to find those who will successfully deal with the problem involved.

For those who are mentally ill or seriously disturbed, the only resource will be the psychiatrist. A psychiatrist is an M.D. who has specialized in psychiatry and passed or who is in the process of passing the American Board of Psychiatry and Neurology. Those affiliated with medical schools or mental hospitals or mental health clinics may be contacted through the institutions. Those in private practice may usually be found in the yellow pages of the telephone directory under the listing "Psychiatry and Neurology." In larger cities they may be contacted through the county mental health association.

The pastor can contact the family doctor with reference to the mentally ill. He may say, "Mr. So-and-so, who is a patient of yours, has been to see me about a marriage problem. Some things she tells me make me wonder if she may need the help of a psychiatrist." Then he reports the unusual behavior and asks the doctor's advice about how to get her to see a psychiatrist or whether he wishes to see her first and then handle the referral himself.

A second source of help is the clinical psychologist. These have Ph.D.'s, or Master's degrees in clinical psychology. Many of the clinical psychologists are primarily trained in giving tests and may not have been trained in counseling and in marriage problems. The fact that they are listed in the telephone directory under "Psychologists" does not mean that they are equipped in the field of marriage counseling or in any other. Neither does certification by the American Psychological Association necessarily equip them as marriage counselors.

A third group of specialists in this field are those who are members of the Family Service Association of America. These are social workers, usually women. The fact that they are women is no reflection upon them as counselors. But many men with marriage problems will not tell their story to a woman, however well trained, and this tendency needs to be taken into consideration. Then too, not every social worker is trained to do marriage counseling. Each must be evaluated on the basis of training and reputation. Information about the person's interest in and training for marriage counseling can usually be obtained from the director of Family Service (located in most large cities) or from other professional people in the community; or the pastor may write to the national headquarters, 44 East Twenty-third Street, New York 16, New York.

A fourth referral source is members of the American Association of Marriage Counselors. These may be found on university or college campuses, in public counseling agencies or in private practice. Members of the Association hold a graduate degree in sociology, education, theology, medicine or psychology, have had at least four years' experience in marriage counseling (one year of which must be under supervision), and have certain qualities of personal integrity and ethics. Information concerning a member's certification as a marriage counselor by this organization may be obtained by writing the national headquarters, 27 Woodcliff Drive, Madison, New Jersey.

Occasionally one finds a physician, attorney or minister who is skilled in counseling in marriage problems, but does not have any of the above certifications. Such people can be investigated only by personal contact and/or experience in referral to them. The real test, of course, is whether or not they get results in holding together marriages that are salvageable and dealing wisely with those which are not.

WHAT RESOURCES ARE TRUSTWORTHY?

There are a few questions which every pastor must ask himself about anyone to whom he refers people with a marriage problem. Apart from satisfying oneself that the counselor will understand the religious person and will refrain from sabotaging his religious faith or practices, the pastor will want assuring answers to these questions:

1. Can the counselor keep confidences?
2. Is the counselor a warm, accepting person?
3. Does he have the patience to work through the various problems involved?
4. Will he have the wisdom to refer the counselees to other professional persons if the need arises?
5. Will he work with the pastor, if need be, in finding the best possible solution?
6. Will he communicate with the pastor concerning his approach or findings?

The first and last of this especially deserve some elucidation.

There are many professional people in our culture who cannot keep confidences. Some pastors are not excepted. I sometimes think that the primary qualification of a marriage counselor is that he can keep his mouth shut. Marriage problems involve some extremely dramatic and interesting, sometimes entertaining, material. The counselor often hears the intimate details not only about the two people involved, but about other people (sometimes in high places) in the community. If he does not have an iron-clad rule not to reveal any of this material, he should not be used as a referral source. Revealing confidential information to any other professional, or to one's own family or trustworthy(?) friends is unforgivable.

The last question, that of communication with the pastor, is an important one. Just because a person has been referred does not remove the responsibility of the pastor to continue to be the pastor. He still has obligations to help in any way that he can.

A letter to a psychiatrist may say: "I am referring Mr. and Mrs. So-and-so to you for help in their marriage problem. Will you please advise me how I can be of help to them or to any member of their family during this crisis?"

If the pastor wishes to tell the counselor how he sees the problem and what he knows about the situation, he may help the counselor get started on the case.

The team approach to dealing with marriage problems is fast being understood between physicians, attorneys and clergymen. Within the limitation of time (each is extremely busy usually), such communication is desirable. A telephone call or a letter may be of help to the persons in trouble, as well as convincing proof to them that the professionals are working together in helping find the best solution.

HOW TO EVALUATE WHICH COUNSELEES NEED TO BE REFERRED

This is probably the most difficult problem the pastor faces. At least, it will require the greatest amount of psychological insight.

If a pastor simply does not have the time or the patience to do marriage counseling, he ought to refer all of those who come to him with marriage problems. He may say to the counselees: "I am not equipped to do marriage counseling, and I can be of best service to you by admitting it and telling you where you can get help."

If he suspects as they tell their story that one of the two is emotionally ill and needs psychiatric help, he may refer them to a psychiatrist or clinical psychologist, if such persons are available.

If the individuals involved are active (especially if they are leaders) in his church, he would do well to refer them, because it is difficult for the pastor to get the completely accurate story from such people. As one church member said to me: "I would have turned to my pastor, but I could not stand to look him in the eye Sunday after Sunday, knowing that he knew what I had done." Another said, "I'm afraid that if the pastor knew our story my husband would never go back to church again." This is particularly true of close friends of the pastor or of his family. Counseling functions best between people who have no other social relationships except the counseling interviews.

Pastors usually will want to refer people whose problems are chronic or so complex that a considerable amount of time will be involved in solving them. It is not always possible to assess the complexity of the problem in the first or second interview. Usually, however, this can be arrived at by getting the answers to the following questions:

> How long has this situation been as it is now?
> How much insight does each have into the problem?
> What is the motivation in seeking help?
> And how flexible are these two people in adjusting to any changes that may be brought about?
> Finally, are they able to afford the other professional help that is needed?

I remember asking Dr. Paul Popenoe once about the advisability of pastors counseling in marriage problems when they had not had a considerable amount of training in counseling. His answer was: "Many marriages could be saved if some person who is sensible, objective and sympathetic would stay with them long enough for them to find a solution." This ought to be of comfort to sound pastors who are located in outlying areas, away from centers where referral sources are available.

HOW TO INTERPRET THE NEED
FOR FURTHER HELP TO THE COUNSELEE

Marriage counseling as a professional practice is only about thirty years old.[1] Few people know either the need for or the possibility of such help. Consequently, most people stagger along in a sick marriage until the situation is so bad that they turn to an attorney, seeking a divorce.

This warrants the advice that many ministers give in premarital instruction: "The one thing that I want you to remember is this. All marriages have difficulties, some very critical ones. If you begin to have trouble, turn to someone for help before the situation gets too bad." Then they would do well to spell out the helping sources that are available, including himself.

When people need to be referred, however, the nature of the help should be explained. Many people think: What good can a marriage counselor do? If we can't solve our problem, I don't see how talking to someone else will help.

[1] Emily Hartshorne Mudd, *The Practice of Marriage Counseling* (New York: Association Press, 1951). See Appendix B for a list of marriage counseling services and their histories.

The answer for the trained pastor is plain: "The first thing you two need is someone to help you understand why you are having such a problem. You need to know, in the light of your own backgrounds, how you got to be as you are and how you can overcome it. This is a job for a specialist, someone who specializes in personality (or emotional) and interpersonal relations problems. This will take time and a great deal of changing on the part of both of you, probably. I know of someone who deals with just such problems."

It should be said here that the surest way to wreck a marriage that is already shaky is to become authoritarian and insist that a divorce not be considered. It is almost like pushing them toward the divorce court. Why this is true, I am not sure. That it is true, any marriage counselor can testify.

The persons referred by the minister have a right to know that the pastor is confident that the referral source is competent, fair, objective and intensely concerned. If he can assure them of these things, they will find out in the initial interviews how counseling works and whether or not they can profit by it.

Even marriages that are comparatively hopeless need an evaluation (or diagnosis) by an expert counselor. The individuals involved in the problem will at least be better able to prevent the same error from occurring in a subsequent marriage. Where one mate wishes to remain in the marriage and the other, for some reason, is determined to break up the marriage, the one who is concerned for the relationship needs to know, for the sake of future reference, why the marriage has failed. Otherwise, loss of self-esteem and unnecessary suffering may be the outcome.

It is the pastor's opportunity and privilege to interpret to people with marriage problems the sources available, the limitations of counseling, the nature of the counseling process, and the choices open to them if they do not find the help sought.

MAKING ARRANGEMENTS FOR REFERRALS, FOLLOW-UPS AND FUTURE CONTACTS

Should the counselee or pastor make the appointment? This question is often asked. The procedure will depend upon two or three factors. Is the counselee mature and reliable enough to call for the appointment himself? If not, it is better that the pastor do it for him. If the counselee is reliable, it will probably be an expression of his own motivation to arrange the appointment. If not, or if the pastor is well acquainted with the counselor, it may be better for the pastor to set up the appointment.

After the appointment is made, it may be well for the pastor to say, "Let me know how you get along; give me a ring." Sometimes this will give the pastor an opportunity to encourage him to continue in counseling or to explain to him that it takes time for a relationship to be built. In some cases, the pastor may see that the referral source is not able to build a satisfactory relationship and that other sources of help must be sought.

Often resistance to counseling is immediately evident, and the pastor may help, because of his trusted role, in showing the counselee that he cannot be both doctor and patient. The counselee may say, "That counselor suggested that we separate for the time being, until we get to where we feel better toward each other; I don't see any sense in that; I want to be with my children." The pastor can say, "Listen, John, this guy had some reason for saying that. He has dealt with hundreds of these problems. Why don't you give it a try? It may help you to see things differently."

If the pastor finds that the counselee does not wish to be referred to some other counselor, he has to face his own alternatives. Sometimes he has to confront the individual with his resistance to help and insist that he face himself as a proud, arrogant person who had rather blame others than work through his own responsibility in the case. In other cases the pastor will have to admit that he does not see any hope unless both will seek professional help.

If they do go to other counselors for help, a pastor may follow up by contacting the counselor or by keeping in contact with the individuals involved in counseling. My own experience leads me to believe that when a referral is made the best results are obtained by assuming that the counselees get the help needed and by treating future contacts as perfectly "normal" rather than continuing to intrude into the counseling situation.

Even though the pastor assumes some responsibility for referral, he need not assume responsibility for the progress in therapy. This will depend on the skill of the therapist, the cooperation of the counselees and numerous other deep and complex factors—perhaps even their own ability to appropriate the grace of God.

HOW TO USE THE SERVICES OF PHYSICIANS

In most American communities, the most completely available resource person is the general practitioner in medicine. Very few communities have a psychiatrist, a social worker or a marriage counselor. But all communities do have a family doctor. He may run fifty to sixty patients through his office in one day and not have time for much talk about personal problems, but he is the family doctor.

All family doctors are familiar with drugs that help people manage their anxieties. Many people who turn to a pastor actually need medical help and do not know it.

An anxious, thirty-eight-year-old wife found herself blowing up and nagging her husband more than usual. She knew that her anger was irrational and that she felt irritable toward the children in a manner that she had not before. Her doctor prescribed a tranquillizer. Soon she told the pastor, "I guess I was just upset. Now I feel much calmer and I am getting along fine with my husband and children. I guess I don't need to come back to see you."

A twenty-nine-year-old man noticed that he was drinking more than usual. It was alarming to his wife that he stopped on the way home from work for a few beers. She began to complain that he might be on the road to alcoholism. His doctor gave him a relaxing drug to take about four o'clock every afternoon. He omitted stopping at the tavern for beer, related better to the family and soon worked out a good relationship with his wife and friends.

A twenty-two-year-old woman was constantly exhausted and could not respond to her husband sexually. Upon being questioned she admitted that she had had a thyroid difficulty in college, but her doctor had told her to come back in a couple of years. She was referred to an internal medicine specialist who discovered that she had a thyroid deficiency. The taking of thyroid supplement relieved her tiredness and stimulated her sexual response.

Often the pastor may do a real service to a parishioner by suggesting that they first check any physical complications with their physician. Many women, for example, resist sexual advances from their husbands because of vaginitis, when the husband may feel that she is merely selfish or cold. Such possibilities should be eliminated in the early stages of counseling. Physicians can treat only those who come to them and those who will tell them the truth about their problems.

HOW TO REFER TO ATTORNEYS

The competent, conscientious attorney is one of the greatest sources of help for family problems. Unfortunately, some attorneys rush through divorce cases or urge couples not to communicate during the divorce proceedings. However, there are many attorneys who are very conscientious about family matters, especially if children are involved.

The minister and the attorney constitute a valuable team in family problems. The minister needs the attorney and the attorney needs the well-trained minister.

For example, a twenty-five-year-old man who had fallen in love with another woman and who loudly proclaimed what a poor mother his wife was to his two children was referred to an attorney. The attorney said, "You are kidding yourself. You do not stand a chance of taking these children away from their mother. Furthermore, you will not get to see the children very often. You can count on the fact that when you get a divorce you have lost your children for life, yet you will be supporting them."

The husband looked at the whole situation afresh and decided against his "love affair." Soon he built a good relationship with his wife and looked upon his "affair" as a foolish episode in his own growth.

The honest attorney will plainly state the facts to his client. Many wives who seek a divorce need to know how to get a "clean" divorce. If the pastor can work with the attorney in helping him to see which marriages seem to be unworkable, or unsalvageable, and which ones by adequate help can be saved, the two may be of real help in solving marriage problems.

If a marriage is unworkable, and the minister is convinced of the fact, he may communicate this to the attorney, and thereby save unnecessary delay and unnecessary expense in court proceedings.

Most attorneys are open to communication about marriage problems. They rightly resent ministers who give legal advice. Usually they do not resent the minister who is trying to help a couple get together if there is hope of saving the marriage. But who is to say when there is hope and when there is not?

WHAT TO DO ABOUT THOSE REFERRED
WHO "BOUNCE BACK" TO THE MINISTER

It is not uncommon for the minister who has referred a couple to find them back in his office seeking help. At this point he must ask himself some serious questions. Is this a form of resistance to change? Was the counselor really unable to give them the help that was needed, or were they expecting too much too quickly?

In some cases it is the duty of the minister to say to the counselee, "You should go back to Dr. So-and-so and give him a chance to help you." A call to the referral source may indicate that the counselees have been too hasty in their decision.

On the other hand, there are some people who are hoping that someone will tell them what to do. When they do hold to such a view, the pastor must insist that they get all of the facts in hand and then assume responsibility for their own decisions. If one wishes to end the marriage and the other does not, the pastor may refer the one who is clinging to the marriage to someone who will help him (or her) to see the underlying motives involved. This may mean referring the clinging one back to the referral source or to some other person in the community. Usually one of a couple can destroy the marriage, if he wishes to. In other words, the pastor must work on the assumption that a workable marriage can be established only when both mates wish to make it so.

If the pastor feels that the person to whom he has referred a couple has jumped to conclusions or given up too easily, his only recourse then, unless other sources are available, is to say, "Let's try a few sessions and explore this problem together. Perhaps the marriage counselor was correct. If you two wish to try your best at this marriage, I shall be glad to do what I can to help you. When shall we sit down together again to talk this over?"

Or if the pastor wishes to refer the couple to another source, he must not overlook the feelings of the first referral source. Even professional people are highly competitive. They often become resentful if one of their clients or patients ends up in the hands of another person. Since it is a fact that one counselor may not be able to relate successfully to a particular counselee, the pastor should take this into consideration. If he feels that the marriage should be saved or that a different type of help should be sought, he must be prepared to incur the displeasure of the person to whom he originally sent the couple.

HANDLING THE RELATIVES
OF THOSE WHO ARE REFERRED

A final, and sometimes difficult, problem facing the pastor is the relatives of the couple in trouble. They often become nosey and belligerent. They will frequently ask for conclusive opinions from the pastor, and then proceed to quote or misquote him profusely. Relatives often set themselves up as authorities on marriage problems. This puts the pastor on the spot.

The pastor must stand by a few basic principles in referring people: (1) He must know something of the source to which he refers. (2) He must insist on his right to advise a couple to seek competent help. (3) He must not profess or claim to know what is wrong, only that something is wrong or the couple would not have turned to him for help.

If a father says: "Why did you suggest that my daughter see a psychiatrist? Do you think she is crazy?" the pastor's temptation may be to flare back with: "She must be or she would not be acting as she is." A better answer is: "I am not competent to judge that. However I do know that psychiatrists do not deal only with the crazy; your daughter is upset and a psychiatrist can help her to evaluate her problem. I'm sure that you want the best possible help for your daughter. That is why I asked her to see a psychiatrist."

Many in-laws have already made up their minds what the problem is, and with a label in hand they advise accordingly. The minister is in a very good position to say that in-laws are not the proper ones to help a couple in trouble and that objective help seems to be indicated.

Some relatives turn against the member of their family who is in trouble. The pastor can sometimes help them to see that patience and understanding is needed while the troubled person finds himself.

The pastor's role is that of adviser, comforter, mediator and guide. He must know when to advise, when to comfort and when to guide. In all cases he will wish to mediate the love and truth of God as he has experienced it.

NINE

WHICH CASES ARE HOPELESS?

As in Chapter VII, we are trying to define *hopeful* in the framework of (1) saving the marriage if possible; (2) saving the individuals if the marriage cannot be saved; (3) saving one individual if both cannot be helped. By *saving* we mean, in this frame of reference, helping the persons involved to find themselves, to become as nearly "whole" as possible, and to find their best possible solution to their marital situation.

Hopeless, then, would mean that the marriage does not seem to be a workable one, that one or both of the mates do not wish to (or cannot) maintain the marriage relationship, and, sometimes, that neither is willing to look realistically at what the situation is.

It is difficult for many pastors to accept the fact that some marriages are hopeless. Their confidence in the grace and power of God, their allegation that "Christ is the answer" and even their exorbitant beliefs in the power of some kind of psychotherapy, may cause them to spend endless hours trying to save a marriage which is destroying one or both of the mates.

What types of cases, then, are to be considered comparatively hopeless and will probably end in divorce or an extremely unsatisfactory marriage?

ONE MATE DOES NOT WISH TO
SAVE THE MARRIAGE

Frank and Frannie, both 30, had been married eight years and had one child, a daughter, 5. He worked at two jobs and spent most of his spare time bowling. She described herself as a homebody but loved to dance. He drank and smoked, and she hated both habits. He had moved out and said that he did not love her anymore and wanted a divorce. She described him as outgoing, needing to be with people, immature, wanting his own way, sensitive and touchy.

Frank said that the trouble dates back to the beginning of the marriage, that she had always wanted to dominate, that she has temper tantrums, has threatened suicide and had broken a picture over her own head in one of her mad fits. He said that he had stayed with her three years longer than the average man would, that she had been a mediocre bed partner, that she had refused to fix meals whenever he brought a friend home, had "run" his mother down and had been unable to get along with any of his friends. Frank said that dancing was the only thing they had in common, and that the only reason he had stayed this long was that he was afraid of what she would do to herself and their daughter.

When I confronted her with his accusation that she would not face reality and that he had repeatedly told her that he had no love left and wanted out of the marriage, she responded with the following statements (extending over two or three interviews): "I just can't imagine myself falling out of love; he is just part of my body." "My father loved somebody else, but he and my mother stayed together." (There was no evidence of "someone else" with her husband.) "I get lonely and have no one to turn to." "His mom says that he works two jobs to get away from me, because I was always unhappy and he could never please me. I told her to her face that it was a lie. Then she said that all men stay out and drink and that I have to accept it." "You said I was dependent, but isn't everyone in love dependent on the one she loves?" "I don't want a divorce; I love my home and my little girl; and besides, I have never prepared for any kind of work. I planned to be a housewife." "He wants me to come back and see you."

This kind of marriage is hopeless, unless both are willing to change. She clings and maneuvers. He withdraws and flees into unreality in order to escape the reality which is at home. His repeated statement was, "I don't believe she can change; she has promised to change many times."

Their minister tried to get him to reconsider his decision to leave; then asked him not to leave until she could get herself together. The latter he agreed to. Later, he left and filed for divorce on the grounds of mental cruelty. She went to live with her folks.

ONE HAS A CHARACTER DISORDER

It is difficult for society in general, and the ministry in particular, to accept the fact that there are some people in our culture who either cannot or will not behave. I refer to the psychopath or sociopath or person who has a character disorder. These people are not mentally deficient. In fact, they are usually extremely bright. Sometimes they will do good deeds, like taking flowers to the sick or assisting people in trouble, called "mimic morality" in their cases. Often they are charming and entertaining, and may even appear to be warm and spontaneous persons.

The characteristics of these people are as follows: They are shallow in their emotional life, forming no deep attachments to anyone; they "act out"—do what they want to do when they want to do it; they use people, are often extremely clever in the schemes they use to maneuver and control others; refuse to accept blame or responsibility for their misdeeds; do not learn from experience, often make the same mistakes over and over; have no insight (except intellectual) into their own problems; refuse to conform to any rules, God's or man's; have a history of defiance of authority: parents, teachers, policemen, bosses, God; develop grandiose schemes for personal advancement and do not hesitate to lie, cheat, or connive—or do anything but honest work—to get what they want.

On the surface such characters can be recognized "as having a preponderance of behavior that is disruptive for society."[1] The areas where such antisocial behavior shows up may be in outbursts of irrational anger, frequent changing of jobs, irresponsibility in getting to work on time, writing bad checks, speeding in automobiles, drinking sprees, lying when he should know that he will get caught, gambling, stealing, refusing to pay bills, sexual episodes without concern for the outcome and conning people into projects which are unsuccessful. The sociopath is the classical con artist. Of course, such behavior as described above may be the results of other types of emotional disorders, but repeated and long-term deviation are indicative of character impairment which the marriage counselor must take into consideration.

[1] Alexander H. Leighton, *My Name Is Legion* (New York: Basic Books, Inc., 1959), p. 127.

Understanding the inflexibility of these persons, and their deceptive façade, is important for the pastor because both in marital and premarital counseling the facts have to be faced. As a noted authority on this type of personality disorder, Dr. Hervey M. Cleckley, says:

> Psychopaths of both sexes, through this appearance of warmth and sincerity, often win the loyal love of a mate who endures repeated outrages in the relation. Though the psychopath may show transient generosity in many small matters, in a crisis and in the continuing pattern of his conduct, a formidable egocentricity emerges. Despite a ready and sparkling display of shallow feelings, particularly in trivial relations, in all his major affective relations there emerges evidence of astonishing callousness.[2]

Perhaps, in time, man will find some way to restore such people to normalcy. At present, the marriage counselor will need the resources of specialists, psychologists and psychiatrists in evaluating the degree of character impairment present and assisting counselees in making realistic decisions. This does not mean that in such cases the pastor will say, "Ditch the gal; she is no good." Some people have a need to take care of a sick mate. The pastor's approach is to help people married to character-deficient persons to look at the total picture, including the welfare of the children, and come up with their own decisions.

ONE IS A SEXUAL DEVIATE

What is normal and what is abnormal between a husband and wife is not easy to decide. All sorts of deviant behavior turn up in a marriage counselor's office. If a man or woman wishes mouth-genital or penis-rectum relations as a substitute for "normal" genital-genital contacts, most authorities would consider this a perversion or deviant behavior. However, as an occasional indulgence, if both wish this sort of behavior, who is to say that it is abnormal? Also, if a couple wish to masturbate together, for reasons which are conscious or not, there is hardly any moral or religious approach that can be made to the problem. In fact, there is no problem with any sort of behavior carried on between a man and wife, if both find it satisfying.

[2] "Psychopathic States," Chap. 28, *American Handbook of Psychiatry* (New York, Basic Books, Inc., 1959), p. 582.

Bergler points out, concerning the relative body positions in the sexual act, that the deciding factor is not whether or not there are divergencies in the way two people enjoy sex: "The same variations become signs of neurosis when there is an inner compulsion to perform them; the difference lies between 'may' and 'must.' "[3] This applies to many problems within the marriage relationships. Mature, informed people are flexible and spontaneous in their interpersonal responses, including sex.

More disturbing situations are presented, however, where either the husband or wife prefers masturbation to sexual union; or finds pleasure in playing sexually with children; or enjoys window-peeping or hurting or being hurt in the sexual act, or prefers sex relations with his own sex rather than with the mate.

A couple was referred by a pastor to a marriage counselor because, as he said, the woman was involved with another man and was suing for divorce.

In the second interview with the counselor the wife asked if all that she revealed would be in confidence. When assured of this, she poured out a history of perverse behavior which she had not revealed to her own pastor because her husband was a minor official in the church. Early in the marriage he had insisted on mouth-genital relations. When she objected to this, he became angry and withheld himself altogether. Twice in the marriage he had insisted on her going to bed with another man while he watched them in the sexual act. Once, following a drinking party, she had succumbed to his suggestion but has never felt the same toward him since.

She had insisted that he seek psychiatric help but he had strongly resented this and refused.

In another case, the man told his wife two months after their marriage that he was homosexual, enjoyed sexual play with men more than with women, but that he did not want a divorce. He carried on normal sex with her with reasonable frequency, but had to spend a night or two a week at a tavern where homosexuals were known to congregate. At the end of three years, and after the birth of a second child, she decided to get out of the marriage and look for a "normal" man. He had sought psychiatric help and had de-

[3] Edmund Bergler, *Unhappy Marriage and Divorce* (New York: International Universities Press, 1946), p. 84.

cided to remain homosexual. His marriage was apparently a front for his homosexuality.

Many other types of sexual failures lead to divorce. In some cases the wife needs to understand the illness aspect of the husband's behavior, so that her own misgivings about herself may be decreased. In some cases she may be able to understand why she chose a sick mate, and thereby prevent a repetition of the bad choice.

ONE IS A CHRONIC ALCOHOLIC

Excessive drinking often enters into marriage problems, but may usually be thought of as a symptom of something wrong within the marriage or within the individual personality of the one involved.[4] A moralistic or religious approach (such as signing a pledge or praying with the counselee), without counseling, usually does very little good. Sometimes, however, problem drinkers who are not alcoholics, can come to see that drinking is costing them more than it is worth by causing unhappiness in the family, and can be induced to leave off alcohol altogether. This approach will usually require the replacement of the drinking experience and its accompanying pleasures with other satisfying patterns of social and emotional experiences. Else the individual finds himself like the man out of whom the unclean spirit was cast: "the last state of that man was worse than the first" (Matt. 12: 43–45).

The marriage counselor may interpret to the nonalcoholic mate the nature of the problem, help him or her to quit "pulling his chestnuts out of the fire," and assist the nonalcoholic to see that alcoholics do not get better with time. They get worse, at varying speeds. Usually the alcoholic must lose his friends, his job, his family and his health before he will come to his senses. If this is true, and the alcoholic will not take steps to correct his condition (other than making empty promises), the kindest thing the members of his family can do is to precipitate a crisis by which he will become aware that he cannot have both his family and alcohol.

What one finds, all too frequently, is that the mate of an alcoholic may be a self-inflicting person who has a need to care for a sick person. At least, the nonalcoholic mate has related to the al-

[4] Thomas J. Shipp, *Helping the Alcoholic and His Family* (Englewood Cliffs, N.J.: Prentice-Hall, Inc., 1963).

coholic as a sick, weak person. If the alcoholic chooses to recover, gears must be shifted and new patterns of interpersonal reaction must be adopted.

If divorce occurs, the nonalcoholic will need counseling to prevent him or her from selecting another sick person as a mate.

TWO PEOPLE WHOSE NEEDS CONFLICT

Ed, 39, an extreme extrovert, handsome and a salesman, was reared in a home where his mother wore the pants and his father, as Ed said, was "the sweetest man I ever knew." His brother ran away from home when he (the brother) was fifteen, because of a conflict with the mother. His father attempted suicide once and an uncle committed suicide. Ed reports that he had to get his mother's permission for everything he did; nevertheless, he says that she was "a bit of dream dust" and that he loved her dearly.

He is now on his third marriage. The first one ended, he said, because he felt called to enter the ministry (but never did) and she did not want to be a minister's wife. The second wife was a stay-at-home who never wanted to go anywhere and who did not like his friends. He repeatedly told his present wife that he did not love her, spent most of his time with his men friends, criticized his wife's housekeeping, claimed that he did eighty percent of the housework and felt that the only reason he stayed with her was because of their six-year-old son. He laughingly reported that he married his wife because she spent two years chasing him.

Leona, his wife, 37, was an extremely capable accountant, interested in art and music, and known among her friends as intelligent and sophisticated. Her father was a very cold, critical, and extremely perfectionistic man who would not sign her report cards unless the grades were above 90; Ed says that "he was the meanest man I ever knew." Her mother did everything for her, never required anything from her, and still insists on seeing her frequently. After leaving home, Leona formed close attachments to three different roommates and leaned heavily on them for emotional support. She reports that she almost backed out the day before the wedding, sensing that he was not deeply in love with her.

Shortly after their baby was born, he decided that he wanted to go to another state to work. When they moved, she had to go to work, as his vocational plans did not materialize. In this period she had a nervous breakdown and was hospitalized and given electric shock treatments. From then on the marriage went from bad to worse. When she tried to get close to him, he would say, "I gave my love to two women and I'm not going to try again." Sexual intercourse occurred about once a month. If she approached him, he became rude and derogatory and insisted that all he wanted from her was a "buddy" relationship.

During their first interviews, Ed insisted that he never saw a person with fewer faults but that he had no desire for Leona and didn't know why. Because of the child he did not want to leave her, if she would accept the fact that he had to have some fun in life. He said that he did not want to fight with her, that ever since his religious conversion at seventeen he had felt that it was not right to express hostility. Leona said that Ed had ridiculed her love, spent money extravagantly and tried to turn her attempts to have a heart-to-heart talk with him into a joke. He flaunted one flirtation in front of her, but claimed that nothing serious had happened. She reports that he said that he wanted "to sin a little." When she replied that he could sin with her, he began saying, "Okay; she's not my wife; she's not my wife."

Ed's most common physical complaint was headaches; Leona's was upset stomach and insomnia.

In the course of trying to solve this problem, Ed was referred to a medical hypnotist because he felt that he would like to find out what made him tick and why he didn't love his wife. Later, he went six times to a psychiatrist. Neither did any good, he and she both said. Whenever the counselor tried to confront him with his sadistic, though lighthearted, behavior to his wife, he contended that he did not love her and never had.

Leona finally got the message. He did not love her, but wanted to maintain a buddy relation while he went his way financially, recreationally and vocationally. As she looked at the possibility of divorce, she had to face her dependency problem which she had never overcome. In the middle of the divorce proceedings period she experienced panic, fear of the future, fear of getting back in the single status and—most of all—loneliness. At times she leaned heavily on the counselor, upon her former roommate and upon her family doctor for tranquillizers and mood-elevators.

Shortly after the divorce, she was able to say to the counselor: "I am not as independent as I thought I was. I didn't believe you when you said that my real problem was dependency. If I am ever going to stand on my own feet and learn to live, it seems to me that it is about time." The hatred of her father loomed in her mind and she came to see that her father had stood somewhat between her and her mother. This angered her, especially because of her need to lean on her mother. Soon she faced her dependency needs, and her stomach trouble cleared up. Ed, at the last report, is going his own way, complaining of headaches every Sunday night when he comes to see the child.

There are many facets to this case. Neither knew his role very well. Both came from difficult family backgrounds. Ed's other two marriages, plus the problems he had with his mother, had set his teeth on edge about close relations with women. However, Leona's needs were for the father she never had, for intellectual companionship, for close affectional (including sexual) relations and for someone to lean on. Ed's needs were for more recreational activity through which he could release his aggression for many superficial relationships (especially with men) and for some freedom to be impulsive and irresponsible. Ed wanted to keep a superficial buddy relationship, but stay married. Leona could not tolerate this, so she got a divorce. A report two years later, from Leona, indicates that they see each other fairly regularly, on good terms, but neither wishes to remarry the other, nor is either close to marriage with anyone else.

Not all marriages where needs are in conflict will end in divorce. In some, however, the needs are so great and the frustration threshold so low, on the part of one or both, that divorce is the only answer. By "only" answer I mean that it is the answer that people in our culture find.

ONE IS EMOTIONALLY SICK

In some cases, where mental illness is involved, two people may have a fairly livable marriage. Reider has said: "Two schizophrenics who marry may get along miserably. Others marry and often get along quite well." He says that the only exception to saying people in one diagnostic category may not get along in marriage with those in another is the paranoid and the hysteric: "I have known few marriages between the male paranoid characters and the female hysterical characters to succeed, by almost any criterion of success."[5] We must remember that the paranoid personality is stubborn, opinionated, perfectionistic, tense, hard-driving, secretive, blames others and cannot accept flaws in himself, and cannot get close to people. The hysteric, on the other hand, is warm and hungry (emotionally), dependent, expressive, subtly manipulative, sensitive, spontaneous, more like a little child. When these two try to live together, they end in expressiveness met by criticism; warmth met by tenseness and secretiveness; manipulativeness countered by stubbornness, and hunger jutting its sensitive head against aloofness.

Whether the paranoid is male or female, the marriage risk is great.

If neither the psychiatrist nor the minister has found a way to save such marriages as are outlined in this chapter, we must face several important questions: What shall we say to these people who must get a divorce? What is the church's attitude toward divorce to be? Can guidance be given to divorced people who are considering the question of remarriage?

I agree with James G. Emerson, Jr., who has made a very thorough study of divorce and remarriage in the light of theology. After facing frankly the fact that a marriage can die, he concludes that "remarriage should be allowed after a divorce":

> This statement is a conclusion placed upon statements in the Bible and the writings of the Reformation. My argument is that not to recognize divorce is to deny the oneness of God's creation. It is to deny that what theology calls "the condition of sin" may have its effects in every area of life. To say that one hates divorce is not to say that divorce does not exist. A decision must be made as to how to deal with that which does exist.
>
> This statement is further based on the argument that a marriage may die spiritually, just as it may die physically. If remarriage can be granted upon physical death, then it must also be granted for spiritual death.[6]

[5] Norman Reider, "Problems in the Prediction of Marital Success," *Neurotic Interaction in Marriage*, edited by Victor W. Eisenstein (New York: Basic Books, Inc., 1956), p. 317.
[6] *Divorce, the Church, and Remarriage* (Philadelphia: The Westminster Press, 1961), p. 164.

Counseling pastors, it should be said, owe more to the counselee than mere assurance or support. If human beings in our culture make their choices of marriage mates, partly on the basis of their unconscious needs; and if these needs are neither recognized nor removed, why should they not make the same mistake again?

The minister will be interested in every facet of causes of bad marriages and will attack these facets from every angle which time and circumstances permit. Better homes in which children may grow up; better premarital education for the unmarried; assistance in the early stages of marital difficulties; more intelligent and more realistic handling of seemingly hopeless cases, and adequate counseling for the divorced so that they will not repeat their mistakes—all of these are the concern of the pastor.

TEN

QUESTIONS PASTORS ASK
About MARRIAGE COUNSELING

In seminars and conferences with pastors, questions come up which need to be answered, and which have not been answered in the previous chapters of this book. The following answers are subject to modification according to the circumstances and depending on the pastor's unique personality and skills in counseling:

Q. Do you ever pray with a counselee? When?

A. Prayer will mean most if it takes place when there is a sincere felt need for it. It should arise out of the situation. At the close of an interview it is appropriate to say, "Would you like to join me in prayer for God's wisdom and help as you two work on your problem?" This should be done only if you feel right and natural about it; it should never be done perfunctorily.

Q. What do you suggest about the counselees' own use of prayer, church attendance and Bible study during their working through a problem?

A. Church attendance is always in order. Bible reading and prayer are not to be recommended to people who are suffering from acute depressive reactions—it will tend to throw them deeper into a depression, because they will feel increasingly inadequate, and if they read the Bible, they tend to pick out passages which condemn them.

In other cases, however, suggestions from the counselor that the individuals pray specifically and daily about certain inner needs which have been brought to the light, such as the management of anger and overcoming of certain temptations, may help. Random praying does little good. Specific mountains (attitudes) within the individual may be removed by prayer. Suggest that they pray about a specific change of attitude day after day until a change occurs.

Q. What if they ask for your interpretation of a particular passage of Scripture, say on divorce?

A. Give the best interpretation you know, in the light of the total revelation of God as you understand it. If the passage they ask about is not apropos to the problems that are being discussed, confront them with the possibility that they may be asking the question in order to avoid looking at themselves and at their present problem. In any case, help them to see that our God is One who knows how complicated human life is and One who will continue to love us if we act conscientiously and sincerely, with the best light we have as we think the problem through.

Q. Is it ever advisable for pastors to charge fees for marriage counseling?

A. Yes, if the interviews run more than a few sessions, the individuals are using more than their share of the pastor's time, and should pay for it. They should pay into some special fund—charity, building, sermon publication and so on—and the pastor should not even handle the money, if it can be avoided, lest he be accused of making money on the side.

There is usually a direct relationship between the financial sacrifice a couple will make to save their marriage and the diligence with which they work at the job of setting things right. Personally, I would not do marriage counseling, over an extended period, without requiring individuals to pay for it in some way. They make more progress if they are paying.

Q. Should you accept gifts from counselees you have helped?

A. I see no reason why gifts should not be accepted. They may be symbols of atonement, relief from guilt feeling or gratitude, or simply an investment in your ministry. If given freely, a gift may be a part of a new pattern of self-giving which all good counseling should inspire.

Q. What about a counselee who wishes to see you while he is seeing another counselor or a psychiatrist?

A. It is not usually expedient for a pastor to refuse to see any person, at least once, who calls for his ministry. However, in this initial interview he should try to determine whether the counselee is offering resistance to his present counselor, cannot relate to him, or is seeking a unique spiritual guidance from the pastor. In case of guidance about spiritual or religious matters, the pastor may see the counselee on a short-term or occasional interview basis. It may be wise to ask the counselee to inform the other counselor of his purpose and something of the content of the interview. It is not wise for a counselee to see two counselors concurrently for the same problem. Besides the probable confusion to the counselee, it does not make for good interprofessional relations. If the counselee insists on changing counselors, coming to the pastor instead of the other counselor, the pastor may suggest that the counselee talk this over with the present counselor before he changes. Under no circumstances should one counselor offer criticism of another counselor.

Q. Should a pastoral counselor take notes during the interview?

A. This is an often debated question among the helping professions. Some say that it hinders rapport. Others that it helps to make it easier for the counselee to talk freely, that he does not feel stared at, and that taking notes lends a professional air of sincere and continuous interest. My own practice for years has been to take notes during most marriage counseling interviews. In the others, I make brief notes of the interview content shortly after the interview ends.

Q. Is it ever permissible to record an interview, on an electrical recording machine?

A. Not unless the counselee knows that the recording is being made. To record an interview without his consent may well be a violation of the individual's right of privacy.

Q. Should you ever visit a counselee in his home during the counseling period?

A. Yes, if there is good reason to do so. It may give the counselor an opportunity to observe the interaction within the family and the physical surroundings of the home, and increase the relationship as one of helpfulness and friendliness. As a rule, however, the counselees should be required to come to the pastor's home; to his study or office, or to an appointed place in the church.

Q. What if the counselee continues to give history, intellectualizes about his problem, or deals over and over with the past?

A. Where intellectualizing and analyzing persist, the counselor may need to become firm and say something like: "This is getting us nowhere. You are going to have to do something about this or worry yourself to death over it. It is not the will of God that anyone should drive himself nuts over a situation. Either change the situation, accept it or get out of it." It may be of value to confront the counselee with the opinion that he is sitting there waiting for you to wave a magic wand or pray for a miracle to get him out of the difficult situation.

Q. What do you do if a counselee spends all of his time talking about the mate's problems and refuses to look at himself?

A. Keep bringing him back to saying what needs within himself are not being met and how he proposes to meet them. In extreme cases, it may be of value to set aside one interview for talking solely about himself; if he departs from that within the interview, remind him that you have agreed that the interview is to be devoted to what he feels and how he reacts rather than to the mate's behavior.

Q. What is to be done when one mate grossly misquotes the counselor to the other counselee?

A. For one thing, remember that this is stock-in-trade. Counselors are frequently misquoted. The worst possible reaction, on the part of the counselor, is to become offended and retaliatory.

Often counselees simply misunderstand. In such cases the counselor needs to clarify what he was trying to say and admit that communication is not easy. We tend to hear what we want to hear, and see things not as they are but as we are. It is appropriate under such circumstances to inquire: "I wonder why she heard it that way," or "What was her purpose in telling you that?" Then state clearly what you were trying to communicate.

In other cases it is necessary to point out that the mate seems to be using the counselor as a club with which he may hit the other counselee over the head. Make clear that the purpose of marriage counseling is not to find out who is most at fault but to understand what each is doing to the other and how they can find a better relationship.

Q. How do you handle anger and resentment toward the counselor on the part of one or both counselees?

A. After you have clarified what they feel and why, if there is a valid reason, they are angry, try to interpret their feelings in the light of what the emotions really mean. The counselor may say: "You thought I had thrown you a curve. Well, if I thought someone had thrown me a curve, I would probably be angry, too. No one likes to be hurt. I understand how you feel." Then try to help the counselees to accept their anger without breaking the relationship. You may be the first human being whom they have met who will not become angry back at them. If they find that hostility will not be met with counterhostility, it may be a very maturing experience.

Q. Do you think pastors ought to do their own marriage counseling or refer to others?

A. It depends on the pastor's training, his personality, and how much time he can devote to counseling. By and large, I think more pastors ought to refer. Marriage counseling is very complex, involving tremendous personality problems, and requires more knowledge and skills than most pastors have. But many pastors do not have resource persons available and have to do the best they can with what they have. This is especially true away from the large population centers.

Q. Should a pastor use an admissions "Data Sheet"?

A. Yes, if he wishes. One like the sample on the next page may save time and accumulate some valuable information: It may be filled in by the counselee before the interview or by the counselor after the interview has started.

Q. What should determine whether you see a couple together or separately?

A. There is special value in seeing the couple together in the initial and in the terminal interviews. Beyond that the answer to this question must be found in such matters as the seriousness of the problems faced, the ability of the two to talk before each other

Personal Data Sheet

Date _____

Name _____

Street _____

City _____ Zone _____ State _____

Residence Phone _____ Office Phone _____

Referred By _____

Martial Status: Married _____ How long? _____
Single _____
Divorced _____ Number of times divorced? _____
Widowed _____

Age _____ Occupation _____

Mate's Name _____ Age _____

Mate's Occupation _____ Office Phone _____

Length of Courtship (from steady dating to marriage): _____

Children: *Name*   *Sex*   *Age*
1. _____ _____ _____
2. _____ _____ _____
3. _____ _____ _____
4. _____ _____ _____
5. _____ _____ _____
6. _____ _____ _____

Your Educational Background   Mate's Educational Background
    Grade School 1 2 3 4 5 6 7 8   Grade School 1 2 3 4 5 6 7 8
    High School 1 2 3 4   High School 1 2 3 4
    College   1 2 3 4 Degree ___   College   1 2 3 4 Degree ___
    Other: Other:

Church Membership: _____ Mate's _____
Religious Preference If Not a Member of a Church _____

Previous Counseling: By Whom? _____
                      When? _____ Number of Sessions _____

and the suspicions of one that he is being "framed." In cases of suspiciousness, we are dealing with a very insecure, manipulative person who will likely feel framed regardless of how objective and permissive the counselor is. In such cases it may be necessary to see him alone until he sees the situation more clearly and then begin with the other. Usually, however, it will be best to see one for fifty minutes and then the other for an equal time; or each for twenty-five minutes of the same hour. Sometimes, at the close of a split session, the two may be seen together briefly for a summary of where they have gotten thus far.

Q. How often and how long should a pastor see a counselee?

A. Usually fifty-minute interviews are the best. To spend two or three hours in an interview, even in the home, is not advisable. More than an hour or so tires everybody concerned and leads the counselees to think that if the pastor hears the whole story he will come up with a solution in one big package.

Once or twice a week is better than three to five interviews a week unless the counselees have come from a distance and are staying in town in order to get help—in such a case daily interviews may be permissible. Some time between interviews allows a couple to work on their own problem in their own way. Then as progress is being made, spacing the interviews farther apart will allow time to see if the couple are really changing and finding workable approaches to their interpersonal problems.

Q. How can you get one counselee to come when he says that it won't do any good?

A. This is a common problem in marriage counseling. One may want help in saving the marriage while the other does not.

One approach is to counsel with the one who wishes help. A second approach is to have her (or him) to come in for one interview so that the counselor may see her (or him) through the mate's eyes. A third approach is for the counselor to contact the reluctant mate by letter or telephone or visit and invite him to come in for an interview in order to get a better picture of why the counselee-mate is troubled over the existing situation.

If none of these work, the pastor may try to help the counselee-mate to evaluate what is wrong, to decide whether it can be accepted and to examine the alternatives to be faced if it cannot. This, in itself, may take a number of sessions. If the marriage must be thrown into a crisis state (such as suit for divorce or separation), before the mate will seek help, all of the alternatives should be faced before a move is made. If a feeble attempt is made, such as a threat of divorce, the marriage gets better for a short time, and they are back where they started.

Q. What do you do when you get "bogged down" on a case and feel that you are getting nowhere?

A. The wisest thing to do is to talk the whole case over with a more experienced marriage counselor, a social worker, a psychologist, a psychiatrist or a pastor who has had more training and experience in marriage counseling.

The second approach, wisest in many cases, is to refer the couple to someone else.

A third approach is to stay with the couple until they pass beyond the plateau on which they find themselves. All counseling goes through stages where the counselee is not moving and appears to be on a sit-down strike. Sometimes it pays to confront the counselee with this fact and to urge action instead of inertia. It takes patience to do counseling, especially marriage counseling.

And, of course, the fee helps keep the counseling moving.

Q. How may I increase my skills in marriage counseling?

A. Most pastors can find colleges and universities where they can audit or enroll in some good courses in child and adolescent psychology, personality development, social psychology, abnormal psychology and counseling. Some of these may even result in clinical experience in counseling. Most modern seminaries have courses in counseling.

Many hospitals and penal institutions have internships for pastors who can meet the requirements. Write the Council for Clinical Training, 25 Massachusetts Avenue, N.W., Washington, D.C., or refer to January issues of *Pastoral Psychology*, Manhasset, New York.

Various agencies such as the American Institute of Family Relations in Los Angeles (5287 Sunset Boulevard) have seminars in which pastors may enroll for orientation in family counseling. It may be helpful to enroll in one of these.

Nothing will take the place of reading. See some of the books in the bibliography and others cited in the footnotes.

Counseling, however, cannot be learned from books. It can only be learned by dealing with actual cases under the supervision of someone who is trained and successful in handling marriage problems.

Q. Are personality tests of value in marriage counseling?

A. It is my belief that their value lies in two distinct areas: evaluating the degree of impairment that one or both has that brings about the marital stress; and as springboards to get quickly into the trait-conflicts which may be causing their problem. In counseling it is unwise to deal with "presenting problems" without some perspective on how much illness or health these individuals have. This, of course, can be judged partly in the initial (called by physicians, the "diagnostic") interview. Psychological tests, it seems, are to some extent a shortcut, a time-saver. Sometimes they are a life-saver.

One of the less complicated tests is the Johnson Temperament Analysis published by California Test Bureau, 5916 Hollywood Boulevard, Los Angeles 28, California (offices also in Madison, Wisconsin; New Cumberland, Pennsylvania, and Dallas, Texas). This may be used to explore how two people differ in personality traits by pastors who do not have a great deal of formal training in psychology.

The most widely used pen-and-pencil personality test is the Minnesota Multiphasic Personality Inventory, published by The Psychological Corporation, 304 East Forty-fifth Street, New York 17, N.Y. This may be of great value in getting a more comprehensive picture of the illness or health of a couple. However, it is distributed only to those who have had extensive training in personality problems and who can provide proof of ability to interpret the test results.

For pastors who have had sufficient training in psychological testing, some of the projective tests such as the Szondi and the Thematic Apperception Test may be useful. The best procedure is to check with a good clinical psychologist for guidance in which tests you are equipped to use.

No psychological tests will take the place of perceptive interviewing.

BIBLIOGRAPHY

Counseling in General

Glad, Donald D. *Operational Values in Psychotherapy*. New York: Oxford University Press, 1959.

The best single book describing the methods of psychoanalysis, interpersonal psychiatry, dynamic relationship therapy and client-centered phenomenology. Extremely useful for the pastor who wishes to orient himself in the various schools of thought in counseling.

Wolberg, Lewis R. *The Technique of Psychotherapy*. New York: Grune and Stratton, 1954.

This work may be of inestimable value to the pastoral counselor, though written primarily for psychiatrists.

Pastoral Counseling

Hiltner, Seward, and Colston, Lowell G. *The Context of Pastoral Counseling*. New York, Nashville: Abingdon Press, 1961.

Unique in that it presents actual interviews of successful pastoral counseling—largely client-centered—in a church setting and shows the relative results. Location is the University of Chicago Counseling Center and Bryn Mawr Community Church of Chicago.

Johnson, Paul E. *Psychology of Pastoral Care*. New York, Nashville: Abingdon Press, 1953.

This book has two chapters apropos to this field; "Marriage Counseling" and "The Pastor and the Family."

McCann, Richard V. *The Churches and Mental Health*. New York: Basic Books, Inc., 1962.

A good survey of recent progress of pastoral counseling as it relates to mental health. Appendix I contains an up-to-date list of pastoral counseling centers.

Oates, Wayne E. *Protestant Pastoral Counseling*. Philadelphia: The Westminster Press, 1962.

An excellent general book on pastoral counseling. The chapter on marriage counseling is a good summary of the whole problem.

Marriage Counseling

Ackerman, Nathan W. *The Psychodynamics of Family Life*. New York: Basic Books, Inc., 1958.

An important contribution by a psychiatrist. Any marriage counselor
can gain valuable insights by reading it.

Carrington, William L. *The Healing of Marriage*. Great Neck, N.Y.:
Channel Press, 1961.

A thoroughly sound discussion of marriage counseling in general, of
real value to the minister, by a physician from Australia who was
president of the National Marriage Guidance Council there.

Johnson, Dean. *Marriage Counseling; Theory and Practice*. Englewood
Cliffs, N.J.: Prentice-Hall, Inc., 1961.

An excellent basic text on theory and practice.

Masserman, Jules H., and Moreno, J. L. (eds.). *Progress in Psychotherapy*. New York: Grune and Stratton, 1958.

Contains some good chapters on marriage counseling by such authorities as Ackerman, Behrens, Mudd and Goodwin. Otherwise it
offers a survey of how psychotherapy is used in the various professions
and in different countries.

Stewart, Charles William. *The Minister as Marriage Counselor*. New
York, Nashville: Abingdon Press, 1961.

Excellent basic book on pastoral marriage counseling within the
"role-relationship" theory by the Professor of Psychology of Religion
and Counseling at Iliff School of Theology, Denver.

Wallis, J. H., and Booker, H. S. *Marriage Counseling*. London: Rout-
ledge and Kegan Paul, 1958.

A good study of the approach of the Marriage Guidance Council of
Great Britain.

Understanding the Family

Bee, Lawrence S. *Marriage and Family Relations*. New York: Harper &
Row, Publishers, 1959.

A college textbook with especially good chapters on "Emotional
Maturity" and "The Meaning of Love."

Bell, Norman W., and Vogel, Ezra F. (eds.). *The Family*. New York:
The Free Press of Glencoe, Inc., 1960.

Articles are by nearly one hundred different authors, mostly sociologists and anthropologists, and present an excellent study of most aspects
of the modern family.

Cavan, Ruth Shonle. *American Marriage*. New York: Thomas Y. Crowell
Company, 1959.

Though planned as a college textbook, it provides some valuable insights into the various problems faced in dating, getting married and
living together.

Chesser, Eustace. *An Outline of Human Relationships*. New York:
Hawthorn Books, Inc., 1960.

A thorough discussion of every phase of the marriage relationship by
an English psychoanalyst. The final chapter, "The Need for Religion,"
is a good presentation of the importance of meaning in modern life.

Eisenstein, Victor W. (ed.). *Neurotic Interaction in Marriage.* New York: Basic Books, Inc., 1956.

These discussions by twenty-five of the top authorities, mostly psychiatrists, in the field of marriage counseling show the relationship between mental illness and marriage problems.

Ellis, Albert, and Harper, Robert A. *Creative Marriage.* New York: Lyle Stuart, 1961.

A valuable book by outstanding marriage counselors, both former presidents of the American Association of Marriage Counselors. The authors are admittedly nonreligious, but the book has much to offer to religiously-oriented counselors.

Fishbein, Morris, and Burgess, Ernest W. (eds.). *Successful Marriage.* Garden City, N.Y.: Doubleday & Company, Inc., 1947.

Discussion of various aspects of marriage problems. An especially good chapter on "Masturbation."

Landis, Judson T., and Landis, Mary G. *Personal Adjustment, Marriage and Family Living.* Englewood Cliffs, N.J.: Prentice-Hall, Inc., 1955.

———. *Building a Successful Marriage.* Englewood Cliffs, N.J.: Prentice-Hall, Inc., 1948.

Both books contain some valuable research on various aspects of family life. Good discussions of what makes for happy marriages.

Levy, John, and Monroe, Ruth. *The Happy Family.* New York: Alfred A. Knopf, 1938.

An old standby by a psychiatrist and a psychologist whose insights are extremely useful to the counselor. The chapter on "How Families Begin" has a good discussion of adolescent behavior.

Mace, David, and Mace, Vera. *Marriage: East and West.* Garden City, N.Y.: Doubleday & Company, Inc., 1960.

The Maces compare marriage customs and concepts of East and West. This will give the pastor perspective on marriage problems in general.

Masserman, Jules H. (ed.). *Individual and Familial Dynamics.* New York: Grune and Stratton, 1959.

An extremely important study of the dynamics of family maladjustments by over twenty-five different authorities. First half of book is particularly valuable because of its careful discussions of masochism.

Ogburn, W. F., and Nimkoff, M. F. *Technology and the Changing Family.* Boston: Houghton Mifflin Company, 1955.

A good study of the modern American family by two top sociologists.

Popenoe, Paul. *Marriage Is What You Make It.* New York: The Macmillan Company, 1950.

Popularly written but containing wisdom that has come from years of counseling at the American Institute of Family Relations.

Sex and Marriage

Capper, W. Melville, and Williams, H. Morgan. *Toward Christian Marriage.* Chicago: Inter-varsity Press, 1958.

Good discussion of sex from the Biblical viewpoint, written for the general public.

Caprio, Frank S. *Marital Infidelity*. New York: The Citadel Press, 1953.
Excellent discussion of infidelity written by a well-known psychiatrist. Presents the view that unfaithfulness "in many instances is a symptom-expression of some basic underlying neurosis."

Cole, William Graham. *Sex and Love in the Bible*. New York: Association Press, 1959.
A comprehensive study of the concepts of both Old and New Testaments, including most passages which pertain to sexual matters.

Derrick, Sherwin Bailey. *Sexual Relation in Christian Thought*. New York: Harper & Row, Publishers, 1959.
A scholarly presentation of the various views of sex from New Testament days to the present by a Church of England clergyman.

————. *The Mystery of Love and Marriage*. Harper & Row, Publishers, 1952.

Van de Velde, Th. H. *Ideal Marriage*. New York: Random House, 1957.
A thorough study of sexual technique by a European physician, who discusses even the effects of perfumes on sexual stimulation.

Background Readings

Emerson, James G. Jr. *Divorce, The Church, and Remarriage*. Philadelphia: The Westminster Press, 1961.
The most comprehensive study of the theology of divorce from a Protestant viewpoint. The author, a Presbyterian, has a very modern, practical, realistic approach.

Maslow, A. H. *Motivation and Personality*. New York: Harper & Row, Publishers, 1954.
Not particularly about marriage problems, but very necessary to the understanding of the self-concept in human motivation. Excellent chapter on "Psychotherapy, Health, and Motivation."

May, Rollo, Angel, Ernest, and Ellenberger, Henri F. (eds.). *Existence*. New York: Basic Books, Inc., 1958.
A heavy, technical, but readable book which shows the importance of finding meaning as a part of a human being's recovery. Excellent introductory chapter on existentialism by Rollo May.

Rogers, Carl R. *On Becoming a Person*. Boston: Houghton Mifflin Company, 1961.
Here is the best of Carl Rogers' thinking. Whether one is nondirective or not, the value systems and concepts of healing methods presented here will be appreciated.

Tournier, Paul. *The Meaning of Persons*. New York: Harper & Row, Publishers, 1957.
Here a Christian, Swiss psychiatrist gives a remarkably readable concept of relationships in counseling and the aims of therapy. Especially recommended are the chapters on "The Living God" and "To Live Is to Choose."

Reference Books

English, Horace B., and English, Ava Champney. *Psychological and Psychoanalytic Terms.* New York: Longmans, Green and Company, 1958.

Hinsie, Leland E., and Campbell, Robert Jean. *Psychiatric Dictionary.* New York: Oxford University Press, 1960.

Hutchings, Richard H. *A Psychiatric Word Book.* Utica, N.Y.: The State Hospitals Press, 1939.

These are extremely valuable assets to the counselor as he reads heavier textbooks and for clarifying his own use of terms. Necessary to communication with other professionals.

Arieti, Silvano. *American Handbook of Psychiatry, Vol. I and II.* New York: Basic Books, Inc., 1959.

Invaluable to pastors who have a broad orientation in psychology.

INDEX

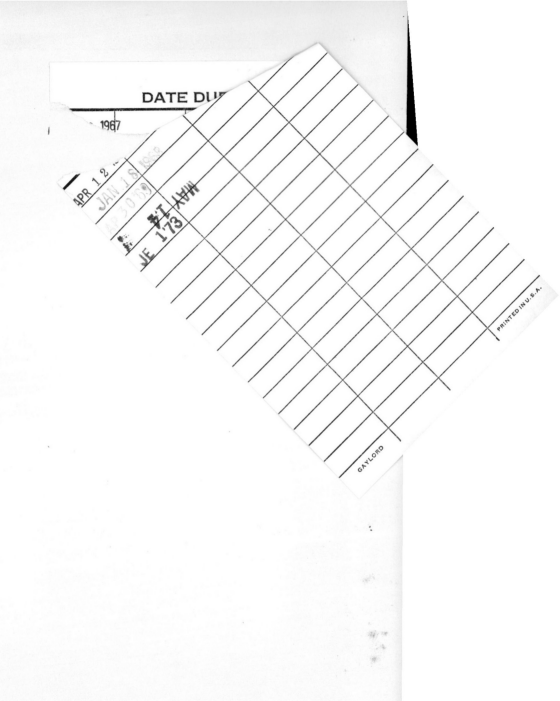